Calm your hyperactive child

Coping with ADHD and other behavioural problems

Dr Sabina Dosani

brilliantideas

CAREFUL NOW

All the ideas here are intended to help you, inform you and provoke your thinking. This is for general information, to give potentially harassed people some encouragement and aid, and should not be treated as a substitute for medical advice from your own doctor or other specialist. Medical science is constantly evolving and changing, and though every effort has been made to provide up-to-date, accurate information, neither the author nor the publisher can be held responsible or liable for any loss or claim arising out of the suggestions made in this book. Everyone is different and we don't know your specific circumstances, or those of your child. If in doubt, you should always consult your doctor for specific advice.

Copyright © Infinite Ideas Ltd, 2008

The right of Sabina Dosani to be identified as the author of this book has been asserted in accordance with the Copyright, Designs and Patents Act 1988.

First published in 2008 by
Infinite Ideas Ltd
36 St Giles
Oxford, OX1 3LD
United Kingdom
www.infideas.com

A CIP catalogue record for this book is available from the British Library

ISBN 978-1-905940-48-6

Brand and product names are trademarks or registered trademarks of their respective owners.

Designed and typeset by Baseline Arts Ltd, Oxford
Printed in India

Calm your hyperactive child

Brilliant ideas

Brilliant features

Each chapter of this book is designed to provide you with an inspirational idea that you can read quickly and put into practice straight away.

Throughout you'll find four features that will help you get right to the heart of the idea:

■ *Here's an idea for you* Take it on board and give it a go – right here, right now. Get an idea of how well you're doing so far.

■ *Try another idea* If this idea looks like a life-changer then there's no time to lose. Try another idea will point you straight to a related tip to enhance and expand on the first.

■ *Defining idea* Words of wisdom from masters and mistresses of the art, plus some interesting hangers-on.

■ *How did it go?* If at first you do succeed, try to hide your amazement. If, on the other hand, you don't, then this is where you'll find a Q and A that highlights common problems and how to get over them.

Introduction

If you've picked up this book, it's probably because your child, or a child you look after or teach, has been diagnosed with ADHD. Perhaps you are a young person who has been diagnosed. ADHD stands for Attention Deficit Hyperactivity Disorder. ADHD is a medical condition affecting the brain that makes it difficult for children to control their behaviour. Children with ADHD find it hard to concentrate, are overactive and act impulsively, without thinking through the consequences of their behaviour.

ADHD children who struggle with inattention have – predictably – a tough time paying attention, but also often daydream, are disorganised and lose things. Children with hyperactivity problems seem to be on the go all the time, into everything and are often squirmy chatterboxes. Impulsive children act or speak without thinking and frequently interrupt.

Although many children have some disruptive behaviour as part of growing up, those with ADHD have behavioural problems that are so all-encompassing and unrelenting that it disrupts their lives and the lives of those around them. They have difficulties in more than one setting, like at home, in school and with friends. These difficulties usually start before a child is seven, but they can be difficult to diagnose in very young children. ADHD is more common in boys than girls and affects between 3–5% of school age children.

ADHD has a few different names. Its older name is attention deficit disorder or ADD. Twenty years ago this term was replaced with ADHD. ADHD is also sometimes called hyperkinetic disorder, or HKD for short. The term HKD is usually used when your child's symptoms are severe and he or she has all three signs of ADHD: inattention, overactivity and impulsiveness.

We've learnt a lot about ADHD and the latest research suggests that it is related to the way that the front part of the brain works. This part is called the frontal lobe, and research suggests that it works more slowly in children with ADHD. This may be because those children don't have enough of certain chemical messengers, called neurotransmitters, which are needed to send messages between the brain and the body. The two neurotransmitters thought to be in short supply are called dopamine and noradrenaline. When a frontal lobe lacks these, it can't react and respond to information appropriately. For a child with ADHD, this means the outside world rushes in with a flood of noise and images, and it is difficult or impossible to decide what's important.

We have come a long way in developing drug treatments. Some drugs aim to increase the amount of dopamine or noradrenaline in the brain. Medication helps most children with ADHD but around one in five will not gain any benefit from it. Other children who do benefit find that the side effects are so unpleasant that they don't carry on. Most children with ADHD also have related difficulties, say with reading or behaviour, that need to be targeted with non-drug approaches.

Although ADHD tends to get better as children get older, young people, their families and teachers need to learn how to manage it on an ongoing basis. Changes to a child's environment at home and in school can improve behaviour. There are also many skills and techniques that adults can learn to deal with ADHD behaviours appropriately and helpfully.

That's where this book comes in. As well as giving you a few ideas about medication, there is a whole menu of ideas inspired by the latest research and clinical experience to help your child. You would be forgiven for thinking they could turn your lively, energetic, inquisitive child into a quiet, retiring one, but the truth is that they won't. Accepting he or she is innately active, full of energy and has a short attention span is probably the best idea in this book. The other 51 ideas will help you, and other adults, manage the difficult behaviour that is often part of ADHD and channel impulsivity into more positive directions. If you try and follow these ideas, you should soon notice improvements in your child's behaviour, angry scenes will be reduced and he or she is likely to get on better both at home and in school. Clinical experience has taught me that ADHD is best managed when young people, parents, doctors and teachers work together towards common goals or treatment targets.

Like managing ADHD, writing a book is a team effort. Many legendary clinicians and researchers at the Maudsley Hospital in London have influenced these ideas and this book wouldn't exist without their work. I've been privileged to work with fantastically skilled teams in both the northern and southern hemispheres, and am indebted to the dozens of doctors, nurses and psychologists who have taught me techniques shared in these pages. I'm grateful to all team players who made this book happen, but especially the parents and young people who have generously shared their inspiring and often courageous stories.

Sabina Dosani

1

Being certain

Many parents wonder how specialists can tell if their child has ADHD. The journey to a definitive diagnosis can be an angst-ridden roller coaster, depressing, confusing and exasperating.

But it doesn't have to be like that. Discover what's going through the professionals' minds when they're deciding for certain.

You may think that it's obvious to everyone from the postman to the lollipop lady that your child has ADHD, but not every child who is overactive, inattentive or impulsive has it. Lots of kids blurt out things they didn't mean to say, or jump from one thing to another, or become disorganised and forgetful.

CALL IN THE PROS

Ideally, an ADHD diagnosis should be made by a professional in your area with training in ADHD or in diagnosing mental disorders. Child psychiatrists and psychologists, developmental paediatricians or neurologists are those most often trained in differential diagnosis. Sometimes social workers also have such training.

Here's an idea for you...

Before you see a specialist for an opinion, keep a diary of your child's ability to concentrate, attention span and activity levels in different settings – for instance at home, with friends and out shopping. Ask a teacher or classroom assistant to keep a similar record for more than one school activity, perhaps during library time, playtime or in a more structured lesson. These records will be valuable in making the diagnosis.

So, you've landed in a professional's office. You're hoping to get a diagnosis. Read on to discover what's going through the pros' minds when they meet you and your child...

Attention deficit hyperactivity disorder is one of the commonest childhood conditions, diagnosed in 1–7% of school-age children who show core symptoms of inattention, impulsivity and hyperactivity. Diagnostic guidelines contain specific requirements for determining when symptoms suggest ADHD. Inattention, overactivity and impulsivity must be a challenge before the age of seven, and continue for at least six months. Above all, the behaviours must create a real problem in at least two areas of a child's life, such as in the classroom, in the playground, at home or with friends.

This means that if your child shows some aspects of hyperactivity, inattention or impulsivity but is doing well at school or has good friends, he or she is very unlikely to be diagnosed with ADHD. This doesn't mean that the ideas here won't be useful; it's eliminating unwanted behaviour that's your goal, not getting a label.

To assess whether a child has ADHD, specialists consider several questions:

- Are these behaviours excessive, long-term and pervasive?
- Do they occur more often than in other children the same age?
- Are they a continuous problem, not just a response to a temporary situation?
- Do the behaviours occur in several settings or only in one specific place like the playground or classroom?

ADHD may be suspected by a parent or caregiver or may go unnoticed until the child runs into problems at school. Given that ADHD tends to affect functioning most strongly in school, sometimes a teacher is the first to recognise that a child is hyperactive or inattentive and may point it out to the parents and/or consult with the school psychologist. Because teachers work with many children, they come to know how 'average' children behave in learning situations that require attention and self-control. However, teachers sometimes fail to notice the needs of children who may be more inattentive and passive yet who are quiet and cooperative, such as those with the predominantly inattentive form of ADHD.

Don't forget: it's normal for all children to have times when they are overactive, find it hard to pay attention or are squirmy and can't concentrate. Because it is so common for children to be like this from time to time, specialists won't make a diagnosis of ADHD unless inattention, overactivity and impulsivity are inappropriate given your child's age.

Try another idea...

Children with ADHD are much more likely to have a host of other medical conditions. Check out IDEA 30, *Double whammy*, to find out the signs to be alert for.

Defining idea...

Hunters in a farmer's world.
THOM HARTMANN, author of
ADHD: A Different Perspective

3

How did
it go?

Q **My son is two and a half. I am worried about him because he cannot sit still and fidgets. He is very strong-willed, into everything and has a mind of his own. He is so different from his sister. He is a lot like my neighbour's six-year-old who was also very boisterous and has been diagnosed with ADHD. I asked my GP if we could get a referral to a specialist but the GP says he is too young. What do you think?**

A *Many parents see signs of inattention, hyperactivity and impulsivity in their toddlers. They often notice their child losing interest in playing a game, or running around completely out of control. But because children grow up at different rates and are different in personality, temperament and energy levels, it's useful to get an expert's opinion of whether the behaviour is appropriate for your child's age. However, experts avoid making the diagnosis in children under five as it is much harder to tell if they have ADHD.*

Q **My specialist has suggested moving to a shared care arrangement with my GP. I'm not sure what shared care means. Could you explain it?**

A *Shared care occurs when secondary care specialists retain responsibility for the ongoing monitoring of children with ADHD after their general practitioner has taken on routine prescribing.*

Q **We've been seeing a clinical social worker and a psychologist who have both been helping my son with his ADHD. I'm not sure what the different professionals do. Who could prescribe medication if he needed it?**

A *Medication should be initiated by a specialist following a comprehensive assessment. Specialists may be consultant child and adolescent psychiatrists, consultant paediatricians with an interest in ADHD or a GP with a special interest (GPwSI).*

2

Cross words

Kids with ADHD often have difficulty controlling their anger. Anger is scary, for kids and adults, as it can mean someone is out of control.

It isn't feeling angry that is a problem, but destructive actions that come after that feeling. Learn the triggers to the feeling, stay in control and live peacefully with anger.

Anger is a feeling. Feelings are not good or bad, they just are. It is healthy to feel angry from time to time, as angry feelings motivate us and protect us against injustice. The suffragettes were angry when they fought to secure women's right to vote.

Shouting rudely, smashing property or frightening people are actions. They are not OK. Many children with ADHD let out their anger using their hands, feet, teeth or by banging their heads against hard surfaces. All children, including those with ADHD, can learn warning signs and triggers to tame their anger before it gets out of control.

Here's an idea for you...

Set some anger rules at home and put them in a prominent place. Anger rules could be something like 'it's normal and cool to feel angry' or 'it's not cool to hurt yourself or anyone else when you are angry'.

During an angry episode many different things are going on:

- Actions
- Thoughts
- Feelings
- The way we communicate anger to others
- The effect of anger on others

We can't always control our thoughts or feelings, but we can control our actions and the way we communicate our anger to those around us. This can seriously lessen the effect of our anger on others. Next time your child has an angry outburst, wait until he has calmed down. Then see if you can encourage him to explain why he felt so angry. Explain you want to understand what was going on. Listening to your child's anger is empowering for both of you. The chances are that you will discover sadness, loss or feelings of helplessness.

FINDING WORDS

Before children can express anger, they need a range of words to use. Develop a feeling vocabulary. Many kids display aggression because they simply don't know how to express their frustrations in any other way. They need an emotional vocabulary to express how they feel, and you can help your child develop one by creating a 'feeling word' word search together. See how many words you can come up with to describe feeling angry and hide them in a word search. These ought to get the creative juices flowing: cross, rage, fury, boiling, hopping mad, crazy, niggly, snappy, fuming, wild, grumpy, sad, irritated, frustrated.

WARNING SIGNS

The trick to controlling angry outbursts is being able to identify anger warning signs. Explain to your child that we all have our own little signs that warn us we're getting angry, and that we should listen to them because they can help us

When we feel stressed or tense, we get angry more frequently to protect ourselves. IDEA 25, *It's all about me*, is packed with relaxation tricks and techniques.

Try another idea...

stay out of trouble. Next, help your child recognise what specific warning signs he may have that tell him he's starting to get upset. For example, 'I talk louder. My cheeks get hot. I clench my fists. My heart beats quickly. My mouth gets dry. I breathe faster.' Once he is aware of the signs, start pointing them out whenever he first starts to get frustrated: 'Looks like you're starting to feel out of control', or 'Your hands are in a fist now. Do you feel yourself starting to get angry?' The more you can help your child identify those early warning signs when anger is first triggered, the better able he will be to calm down and learn to regulate his feelings.

Children with ADHD will appreciate it if you suggest a few ways to let anger out safely:

- Hitting a large cushion with a rolled up newspaper.
- Pushing hard against the wall with flat palms.
- Screwing up old newspaper.
- Scribbling with crayons.
- Tearing up pages from an old phone book.
- Running to the end of the road or garden and back as fast as possible.
- Stamping feet loudly outside.

I see myself as an intelligent, sensitive human, with a soul of a clown which forces me to blow it at the most important moments.
JIM MORRISON

Defining idea...

How did it go?

Q It's not my son's anger that's the problem. It's my own. I know he has ADHD but when he makes a mess of the place, I just lose it. I end up shouting at him and sending him to his room. Then I feel guilty and he skulks about as if he's scared of me. What can I do?

A You're not alone, and the fact that you have tried and are asking for help means you are far from being a bad parent. You're losing it not because the room is a mess, but because of the view you take of it. Try focusing on your ability to help him, which will help you stay calm. As soon as you feel your anger rising, ask yourself these questions. What's my goal? (to get this room clean, to stay calm), what is the next step I need to take towards that goal and what am I already doing, and what could I do more of? All parents lose it sometimes, so don't be too hard on yourself.

Q We've been trying to develop an emotional vocabulary but my daughter still struggles to explain how she feels when she is cross. I'd really like to understand what is going on for her. What can I do?

A Drawing a picture and talking about it can help if she's struggling to find words. Try asking her to draw the angriest picture she can.

3

Flexible friends

Many children with ADHD find it difficult to change plans when facing setbacks. Discover how to help them be more adaptable to changing conditions.

Kids with ADHD often need to know what's going to happen at any given moment. The trouble is, life's just not that predictable.

Having a daily routine helps children with ADHD plan for predictable frequent transitions, like going from home to school. At holidays, weekends, parties and other special occasions these day-to-day routines are thrown out and ADHD kids are more likely than ever to become argumentative and tearful. They also find transitions from one activity or setting to another equally hard to handle for exactly the same reason.

Children without ADHD often appreciate a five-minute warning before being changed from one activity or caregiver to another; those with ADHD need much more preparation than that. Many parents find that if their child does not have at least ten minutes' warning before a transition, they are unable to shift their attention.

Here's an
idea for
you...

Encourage your child to think up different ways of busting boredom. You can make this into a game, where he thinks of as many as he can, and you write them down. They can go on his bedroom wall, and when his chosen activity isn't available, he can go and look at the list. Alternatively, he could make a collage or drawing of things to do when he is bored which can be displayed in a prominent place.

Prevention is easier than cure. Pick your moment and have a chat about flexibility. Help your child understand what being flexible means. It is easier if you pick an example from daily life, like 'there's more than one answer when you ask me what's for dinner. It won't always be fried chicken and chips, sometimes it will be cauliflower cheese'. Once a child can understand that there are different possible responses, try explaining that there is also more than one solution when he feels bored at the weekend. Try saying something like, 'sometimes we can go to the museum and see the T Rex, but sometimes we can't and you could stay in and draw it instead'.

People who are less flexible imagine what they think will happen. They play this imagined best outcome through their mind like a film. When it doesn't happen, it feels catastrophic, like not being able to go to a film premiere when you already have the red-carpet dress and the shoes. When real life and the imagined script mismatch, they feel angry, confused and frustrated.

A good strategy is to make plans for specific times when children might need to be flexible. For instance, have a variety of play plans that are dependent on the weather. So instead of asking your child, 'what shall we do at the weekend?', try asking, 'what shall we do at the weekend if it's raining?' and 'what about if it's sunny, what could we do then?'

Being skilled in a range of relaxation techniques can take the stress out of disappointments. Check out IDEA 25, *It's all about me*, for an assortment.

Try another idea...

Role playing can help children see how other people see them, and gives them a chance to try new responses and behaviours in a safe setting. Get out the dressing-up box and role play these scripts with your child. Experiment with what children will say to other children or adults in potentially frustrating scenarios. Encourage them to take turns at playing the adult while you play the child and then swap roles. The aim is to not only identify what they might say to the other person, but also what they could say to themselves. For instance, if your child usually plays football on a Saturday morning, but the game is cancelled due to bad weather, you could role play that happening. He might then say to himself, 'never mind, we can do that another time'.

An oak and a reed were arguing about their strength. When a strong wind came up, the reed avoided being uprooted by bending and leaning with the gusts of wind. But the oak stood firm and was torn up by the roots.
AESOP

Defining idea...

How did it go?

Q **My daughter gets confused and frustrated easily. Every other Friday, she stays with her father. She gets herself into a terrible state and is upset by the change to her usual after-school routine. We have tried to role play and plan ahead. She seems to get the idea at the time but when he arrives, she still gets stressed. What do you suggest?**

A *New skills take time to acquire. Think of yourself as the producer of the Friday Night Show. You wouldn't go live on air without a rehearsal, so don't leave real life to chance. Plan a dry run. It sounds as if you are already giving her advance warning, so why not make a game out of a difficult scenario? Invest in a clapperboard, cues and routines, call her from the dressing room five minutes before she is ready. Go through this routine before her dad comes.*

Q **My son loves playing cricket. He gets very upset when he thinks the umpire has made a mistake. Last Saturday, this happened and he got very angry, shouting at the umpire and arguing back. It doesn't wash with other parents to say he has ADHD. What can I do?**

A *Prepare him for this. Talk to him and explain that grown ups are 'allowed' to make mistakes. Accept that he has a need to have a sense of control during a game like cricket and try to keep this in mind when other parents comment.*

4

Move it

If the only exercise your child gets is pushing her luck, then she needs to get moving. Studies show that exercise has a positive effect for children with ADHD.

Aim for forty minutes per day of exercise for your child. This might sound daunting, but you can split this into two twenty-minute sessions.

Exercise has powerful effects on all our brains. A brain is essentially a colony of ten billion interconnected cells that communicate. Between each cell there are spaces called synapses. A synapse is a sort of junction between two brain cells, where the end of one almost touches another. Imagine you're talking to a friend and you're both on the bus. Easy, you just turn and speak. But when you want to let your boyfriend know you'll be late because the bus is stuck in traffic, you use your phone.

Cells use an equivalent of your mobile phone to communicate with each other across the synapse. Electrical charges are used to communicate inside brain cells. But electricity doesn't carry across the synapse, just as your voice doesn't carry outside the bus. So, while you'd use your phone, brain cells release chemical communicators. These chemical communicators are usually stored in little capsules called vesicles and swim into synapses when needed, carrying their message to the next cell. These chemical communicators are called neurotransmitters. Nobody

Here's an idea for you...

Bouncing on a trampoline can be useful for children with ADHD; it helps develop their sense of balance. During especially hyperactive days, encourage children to bounce off excess energy after school. This can help them focus on homework or sit through dinner.

knows exactly how many neurotransmitters there are, but at the last count there were over forty. They carry different messages. Some get their part of the brain turned on and excited, others put a damper on things.

Aerobic exercise increases levels of the neurotransmitters dopamine, serotonin and noradrenaline. These are necessary for emotional regulation, the ability to focus, mental alertness and calmness. Conversely, a deficiency in neurotransmitters can cause depression, mood swings, irritability, anxiety, attention problems, stress and sleep problems.

In 2001, a University of New York study showed the positive benefits of exercise on ADHD children. The study group – ADHD children between the ages of five and twelve – participated in forty minutes of intense exercise five days a week. The children involved showed a significant improvement in behaviour over the duration of the study. The benefits of regular exercise include being less hyperactive, less impulsive, more co-operative, having reduced aggression levels, better sleep patterns, an improved appetite, being more even-tempered, having fewer angry outbursts and better team-playing skills.

Although overactivity is a key feature of ADHD, many children with it are reluctant to exercise. Often parents take their children swimming and find that the child with ADHD loses interest quickly, only to be squirmy and fidgety on the return journey while other kids are relaxed and pleasantly worn out. Scientific research suggests that children with ADHD may be biologically resistant to exercise. This is because their stress hormones do not increase during exercise as much, so they may require more exercise than other children to reap the same benefits.

Children need the right fuel to have enough energy to exercise. Check out IDEA 33, Food for thought.

Try another idea...

To be most effective, exercise needs to be vigorous. Children as young as four can and ought to do forty minutes a day of exercise. If your child is old enough to have been diagnosed with ADHD, she's old enough to exercise for forty minutes a day, in two twenty-minute chunks if necessary.

Next time you need to make a short car journey, ditch the wheels and try walking with your child. This not only helps her achieve her exercise target for the day but also sets an important example. Expect some resistance the first time but stick to your resolve and insist that she walks with you for at least fifteen minutes. Once she can do this, ramp it up by increasing the walk by five minutes every day. Point out interesting things and make walking fun – for example, by playing poo trail...

Young kids are fascinated by faeces. While you walk, give your child special responsibility for finding out which animal's footsteps you are following by identifying their poo. Cowpats, rabbit droppings, pigeon splatters and doggie doo bring out the best in kids usually bored on a walk. If you introduce a bit of competition – 'who'll be the next to spot a poo and tell everyone what it is?' – you'll be surprised how far those little legs can go. Ultimately you need to help your child build up to vigorous exercise that gets the heart racing or breaks a sweat.

Lack of activity destroys the good condition of every human being, while movement and methodical physical exercise save it and preserve it.
PLATO

Defining idea...

How did
it go?

Q **My son is full of nervous energy. We were wondering about getting him involved in some sort of sporting activity but worry that he will not fit in and might even get bullied. He seems a bit clumsy and I don't think he would be good at ball games. What do you suggest?**

A *Non-competitive exercise like skateboarding or inline skating can help build self-esteem. Regular walking, cycling and swimming are good provided he keeps up a fast pace. You mention he is clumsy – difficulties co-ordinating and performing certain movements may be due to a condition called dyspraxia, which is commoner in children with ADHD. Speak to your GP about a special dyspraxia assessment.*

Q **My son enjoys karate and has a red belt. He trains three times a week and loves it. It doesn't seem to affect his hyperactivity much, if at all. What do you recommend?**

A *Martial arts are excellent for improving focus. How fantastic that he has the discipline to achieve so highly in karate; it's clearly something he enjoys and excels at and should be encouraged to continue. Whatever additional activities your son is doing, he needs to break a sweat or get breathless. Getting him to walk, then run, to his karate class and back may be an idea you could try.*

5

What's not wrong?

It's human nature to notice when things have gone wrong. Noticing the bad stuff 24/7 has instantaneous, forceful and long-lasting negative effects.

Discover the secret to focusing on the good times, with a game to help cultivate an attitude of gratitude. Playful positivity helps fight the effects of stress and soothe frazzled nerves.

All problems have exceptions, times when the problem could have happened but somehow did not. This idea comes from Solution-Focused Brief Therapy, a short-term goal-focused therapeutic approach which helps people change by constructing solutions rather than dwelling on problems. The ability to articulate what change will be like is often more important than understanding what led to the problem. The approach was developed by Steve de Shazer and Insoo Kim Berg and their colleagues at the Brief Family Therapy Center in Milwaukee.

Here's an idea for you...

Children with ADHD need more immediate consequences for their behaviour than children without it. A child without ADHD may require praise a few times a day when they have done something really well. Kids with ADHD need much more frequent feedback from you whenever they have got something right. Aim to catch your child doing something right and comment on it at least once an hour when you are together.

Looking for those times when the problem did not arise when it would normally have, provides clues to what your child and you can repeat until you are satisfied that things are better. Even when children with ADHD don't have good solutions that they can repeat, most have recent examples of exceptions to problems.

Barbara Sher, an occupational therapist with many years of experience working with parents, teachers and children across the globe, has developed a game called 'what's not wrong?'. It helps you and your child with ADHD get a sense of balance during the highs and lows. In this game, participants take it in turn to name something that is not wrong. For example: 'I didn't get told off at school today', 'we didn't fight at playtime', 'Mum made my favourite dessert today' and 'my dog didn't have to be put down'. A variation on this is to ask your child to share something good that has happened at the end of each day.

ASKING QUESTIONS RATHER THAN TELLING CHILDREN WHAT TO DO

Questions are important. This game helps you ask in a curious, non-judgemental way and avoids direct challenges or confrontations.

THE FUTURE IS NEGOTIATED AND CREATED

The question used in this game is almost always focused on the present and future. Therefore, rather than emphasising and dwelling on past mistakes, bad luck or ordeals, focusing on what is going well and what works is much more productive and empowering than focusing on past events or guessing about what might have been the origin of the problem.

GENTLE NUDGING TO DO MORE OF WHAT IS WORKING

Once you have discovered what's not wrong and identified some times when a particular problem doesn't happen, you can gently nudge

Children with ADHD need more positivity than others, and are also more likely to have low self-esteem. Find out how to kick it up a notch in IDEA 22, *I like that.*

Try another idea...

Life is a continual process of savouring the ups and working out the downs. It takes practice to appreciate rainy days as much as days when the sun is shining. Nothing is so small to recognise as something that is not wrong.
BARBARA SHER, occupational therapist

Defining idea...

19

Here's an idea for you...

Kick this up a notch by giving compliments. Validating what your child is already doing well encourages change while giving the message that you understand and care. Compliments can punctuate what he or she is doing right when telling 'what's not wrong'.

your child or other people in the family to do more of what has previously worked, or suggest trying changes they thought they would like to try.

CHANGE IS CONSTANT AND INEVITABLE

As the Buddhist teaching says, stability in life is an illusion; life is constantly changing and we are always changing. Some changes are more noticeable and apparent than others. It means that the more we look for small changes, the more we will notice them. Therefore, noticing and paying attention to small changes can set in motion more and more changes. Since we are all changing, the focus is on how to direct our attention to the more positive changes that are already occurring.

Here's an idea for you...

Reflecting on what went right not only gives us encouragement, but also creates harmony. It's like filling a garden with flowers instead of worrying about weeds. Plant enough flowers and you'll choke out all the weeds.
VENERABLE AJAHN BRAHM,
Buddhist abbot and expert on harmony

Q **We tried this at home and found it very difficult not to end up dwelling on what has gone wrong. It's almost inevitable that my son's bad behaviour outweighs the good and it's hard to be positive. What do you suggest?**

How did it go?

A *Firstly, go easy on yourselves. Just making the change and playing this game is a sign of your commitment to doing things differently and looking at life in a new way. Change isn't always easy. Pay particular attention to the language you use. 'Johnny didn't smash up the living room' is going to be less effective than 'Johnny played nicely with Jordan for an hour while I did the ironing'.*

Q **This all sounds very simplistic. Does focusing on what's not wrong really work?**

A *Research shows that many different approaches to ADHD 'work' and arguments about which approach is better than others are often spurious. A number of studies conducted at the Brief Family Therapy Centre in Milwaukee reported success rates of 70% and above.*

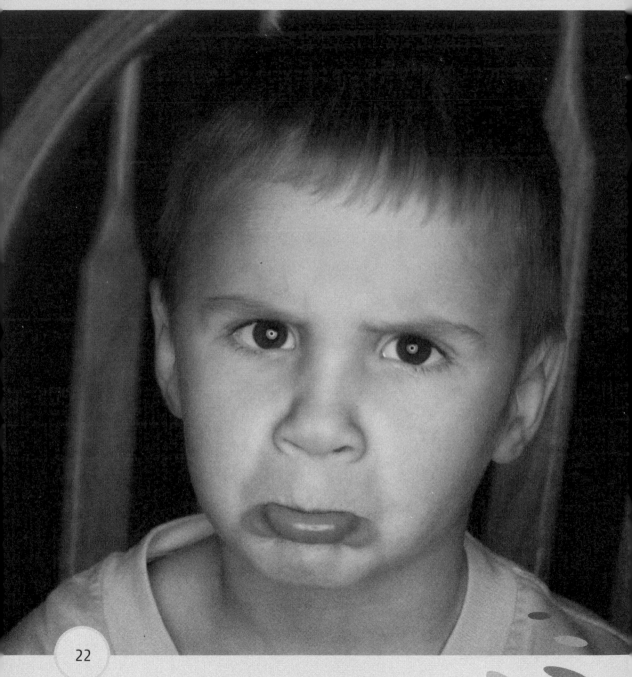

6

Time out

You've seen it used on television, but can't make it work at home? Here's how to make time out work for you and your ADHD child.

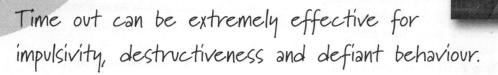

Time out can be extremely effective for impulsivity, destructiveness and defiant behaviour.

At its simplest, time out means sending your child to a boring place for five minutes. Kids hate missing out on fun and so learn to do anything to avoid it – and this means they stop doing the bad things that land them there. The knack is to use time out calmly, in a planned way, for specific behaviours. There are guidelines you can go by.

Time out needs to be used to target the specific things which your child does that you need to change. In the trade we call them 'target behaviours'. For example, if you are going to use time out when your son or daughter hits people, don't use it for swearing as well. Once you've decided to use time out for a target behaviour, you'll have to stick to it.

Here's an idea for you...

The way to sell time out to your child is to tell him time out is something your family is introducing to help him behave better so he can feel better about himself. Explain how time out works calmly, for instance saying 'you'll be sitting in the bathroom for five minutes' rather than yelling 'you've driven me crazy and will have to sit in the garden shed and not come out for ten years'.

Time out rooms need to be boring and safe. Guest bedrooms, bathrooms, utility areas and laundry rooms are usually suitable. Your child's bedroom is not. Whichever room you select, empty it of breakable objects or anything that looks like it might be fun to play with. If you live in a small or open-plan home, use a special chair for time out. Put it in an area away from other kids and any possible activities.

The length of time children ought to spend in time out depends on their age. If they're between three and five years old, three minutes is enough. When they're five to ten years old, five minutes is fine, and if they're older than ten, go for ten minutes. Quality rather than quantity is key. Longer time outs are no more effective than shorter ones. It helps a great deal if you put a clock in the time-out room that kids can see. Show them where the big hand will be pointing to at coming out time.

Once you've chosen your time-out target behaviour and location it's time to tell your child. The best time to do this isn't when you're angry or to add colour to a lively argument, but when everyone is calm and getting on reasonably well. It will all go horribly wrong if you use time out as a threat, however. If you say, for instance, 'if you throw the hamster downstairs one more time, you'll have to go to time out', it gives a child an extra chance to do something bad.

Parents who use time out most successfully are those who plan ahead. When a child does a target behaviour, time out follows like night follows day. Those parents who are less successful with time out tend to be inconsistent; for example, letting their child off sometimes and at other times losing it and shouting, 'you look like someone who wants to be in time out'.

Time out won't work if you use it in isolation. Use it in conjunction with praising and rewarding behaviours you want to see more of.

Using time out at home and it's working well? Great, but what do you do when you're out and about? Some parents get round this by making a note of any misbehaviour usually resulting in time out, and then sending the child there immediately when they get home. The problem with this is that there is inevitably a delay between misbehaviour and time out, and your child may continue to play up during the outing, knowing he will be going to time out anyway when he gets back. If you're in a shopping mall, park, leisure centre or place of worship, there will usually be a safe quiet area, like a mother and baby room or even an outdoor bench where your child can sit quietly for five minutes. If you're in a restaurant or fast-food outlet, a baby-changing area will be your best bet for younger children, but you may need to take an older child outside for five minutes.

Try another idea...

Time out works best when combined with praise. Learn how to give effective praise in IDEA 22, *I like that*.

Defining idea...

When my kids become wild and unruly, I use a nice, safe playpen. When they're finished, I climb out.
ERMA BOMBECK

How did it go?

Q **My son calls out 'how many more minutes?' about four times a minute. Because I have to keep going to tell him, he ends up getting more attention than when he's not in time out. Where do I go from here?**

A *You're right that paying him extra attention will make time out counterproductive. There are several things you can use or do instead. Use a kitchen timer which clicks down the minutes, get him to watch the sand running in an egg timer, show him on the clock and tell him you will tell him when the time is up, and not before.*

Q **My daughter screams and has tantrums during time out. What can I do?**

A *I know it's tough, but the best strategy is to ignore her. Don't start counting minutes in time out until her tantrum is over. Tell her she has three minutes in time out and you'll start timing when she's quiet. Once she has learned that silence gets her out of time out quickly and that tantrums just extend it, she'll stop screaming.*

7

Indecent exposure

You don't need me to tell you that ADHD is 24/7. Many parents are able to manage their child's symptoms at home but get stuck when venturing out of comfort zones.

It's easy to feel you can't do as much as you can at home when you're in the dentist's waiting room, the library or at a formal tea party.

Managing in public places can be challenging, but get it right and you'll have time to enjoy fun, games and the excitement of childhood, rather than be burdened by the annoyance of ADHD. Time for some straight talking. Unless you have a repertoire of techniques to manage the challenging behaviours associated with ADHD, you're saying it's OK to misbehave outside home.

Use these small but powerful techniques to manage your child's behaviour when you are out and about. If these choices become part of your busy everyday existence, you'll be able to focus your energies on managing your child's behaviour on the move and reduce the stresses that used to be associated with them. The sooner you start, the sooner you'll feel confident about going out with your child with ADHD. Wherever you are, when you are faced with behaviour that is unacceptable, the trick is taking immediate action. These ruses will help.

Here's an idea for you...

Before going into a public place, like a shopping centre or library, stop for a moment and calmly remind your child of the rules. One smart way of doing this is giving him three rules to remember. Choose the three most commonly broken ones and get him to repeat them back. Be clear about what rewards he will earn for sticking to each rule. Stickers or healthy snack food like raisins are good portable rewards for public places. Show your child the reward before you go in.

THE SHOPS

Before going into a shop, explain the rules. Tell your son or daughter what is expected, offer a reward for complying with the expected behaviour and a consequence for not complying. 'We are going into a shop for twenty minutes to buy a present for Aunty Elisabeth. You are not allowed to touch anything or run about, but you can look at things and help me select a present. When you have been good in the shop, I will let you choose the wrapping paper for the present. If you touch things, or run about, you will have to go to time out.' After a clear command like this, ask your child to repeat back what you said.

THE CAR

Again, before a car journey, be clear about the rules. Whether this means no fighting in the back, no wriggling or something else, it is important to be clear and have your child repeat them back. If the rule is broken, pull over and don't drive for ten minutes. Explain that this is an in-car 'time out' and that every time a rule is broken you will have a boring time for five minutes in the car. Don't listen to the radio or engage in any conversation for these five minutes, just pull over and hold your ground. Sit back and try to look relaxed, even if you are feeling tense. This shows your child you mean business.

GOING TO SOMEONE ELSE'S HOUSE

It's harder – but not impossible – to enforce limits when you are at someone else's house. Stand your ground. If behaviour is unacceptable, speak up and tell your child that you expect him to behave just as well as he does at home.

Children who are confident and who receive a lot of appropriate praise are likely to behave better when they are out. Check out IDEA 51, *Complimentary therapy,* for ways you can crank up both praise and confidence.

Try another idea...

IN A RESTAURANT

Children with ADHD can find restaurants a real chore, especially ones which are more adult than child friendly. If you find yourself going to one of these, it helps to be prepared. Together with your child, make a pack of activities to take, like colouring or activity books, small electronic toys and whatever else holds the attention and can be played with discreetly at the table. Again, be clear about your expectations and if your child breaks the rules, tell him you are taking him to sit in the car for five minutes to calm down.

On the whole, human beings want to be good, but not too good and not quite all the time.
GEORGE ORWELL

Defining idea...

How did
it go?

Q **I dread taking my six-year-old son shopping. He's into everything, runs away and charges around like a little fruit loop. How can I get to grips with his impulsivity?**

A *It sounds as if time out would work, but instead of waiting until you get home, take time out into the shops with you. Before your next trip, reinforce the rules, being clear about what you do and don't expect. If he misbehaves, tell a shop assistant that you need to sit somewhere quiet for five minutes. Changing rooms or a lounge area, in bigger malls, are ideal. Sit together quietly; ignore his questions and attempts to draw you into conversation. You might need to repeat this, but chances are you won't need to do it more than a dozen times.*

Q **When we go to friends' houses, my son is much more hyper. He really plays up to an audience and shows off with rude language. I feel so embarrassed and don't know what to do. What do you suggest?**

A *I'm not surprised you feel embarrassed. But you can use that emotion to motivate you to change how you respond to your son, so that he doesn't perform to an audience when you are out. Next time he swears or misbehaves, tell him calmly that you want him to behave as he does at home. If he doesn't, cut the visit short and drive him back. You won't have to do this often.*

8

Stars and stickers

Want your child with ADHD to be a little star? A packet of little stars could do the trick.

Star charts can be incredibly useful for correcting behaviour or encouraging behaviour you'd love to see more frequently.

At their simplest, you can use a star chart to reinforce the behaviour you'd like to see more of, or to extinguish behaviour you'd like to see the back of. For instance, your child waiting his turn at dinner, reading quietly in bed or completing homework equals one star on the chart.

Sticker charts can also be used to increase attention span. Little children usually get what they want straight away because parents rightly respond quickly to a crying baby or fretful toddler. Older children can be taught to wait and you can use star charts to increase their ability to wait their turn or extend their concentration span. Start by timing how long your son or daughter can typically play quietly or concentrate on homework. This may only be a few minutes. After school, set the kitchen timer or your mobile phone for the amount of time you know he or she can definitely stay still. Award a sticker if the time is reached.

Here's an idea for you...

Star charts work well with younger children, but you can get even more out of them by introducing a trading system. An agreed number of stars can be cashed in for a treat. Having something tangible to work towards can be a powerful motivator. Run it by your accountant or at least a friend with financial nous before you hand out half the solar system!

Over the next few days, your child might collect a sticker for each of the following, for example:

- Doing homework for five minutes
- Playing with his brother for ten minutes
- Reading quietly for five minutes
- Waiting his turn on the PlayStation for ten minutes

After a few days, he'll have the idea of collecting stickers and will be motivated to do things that mean he can have one. By day four of using the sticker chart, add a minute or two to the length of time you expect him to be quiet or co-operative. Many parents find it helps to do this at the same sort of time every day, like immediately after school or before dinner. The key to success is not to lengthen the time until he has been successful for a shorter time on at least three or four occasions.

You can get more value out of star charts by encouraging children to swap a certain number of stars for a tangible reward. Many parents feel uncomfortable with the idea of 'bribing' their child to do something. But using rewards adds to the child's excitement and helps build towards a sense of achievement when the chart is finished. Rewards shouldn't be huge; they should be treats that mean a lot.

Some parents worry that all the treats that are swapped for stars are spoiling their children. Often one parent feels rewards should be less material and that a few words of praise ought to be enough. Children with ADHD often need more powerful rewards than other children. Stars, stickers, tokens, points and treats like little toys motivate them. Many parents of children with ADHD worry that their child may miss out on more subtle rewards that come from within, like feeling satisfied with a job well done, the warm glow associated with finishing a drawing or pride at completing a school project. However, kids with ADHD are less motivated by these internal feelings than they are by the prospect of earning stars to exchange for a plastic Bart Simpson or Buzz Lightyear.

Stickers and stars are just one way of recognising good behaviour and motivating your child. Praise is also important. Learn how to boost your verbal muscle in IDEA 22, *I like that*.

Try another idea...

It is not giving children more that spoils them, it's giving more to avoid confrontation.
JOHN GRAY, *Children are from Heaven*

Defining idea...

How did it go?

Q **We started using a sticker chart to help my daughter be good at mealtimes. It worked for a few days, but now she's all over the place again, getting up, picking at her food, interrupting conversations and behaving in unacceptable ways. What can we do?**

A *It sounds as if you are trying to correct too many behaviours at once. I'm not sure exactly what you want your daughter to do, so chances are she's not sure either. Don't worry, lots of parents make this mistake. Spend a few minutes writing down exactly what you mean by 'being good at mealtimes'. Maybe you want her to stop playing with her food? Perhaps you want her to sit at the table until everyone has finished? Alternatively you might allow her to leave if she asks permission first. How do you feel about her leaving after the main course and returning for dessert? Think these things through, and once you are clear about what is important, stick to it. Explain to her what she needs to do to earn a sticker, remind her before meals and perhaps get her to do a drawing of being good at mealtimes to keep with the sticker chart.*

Q **Until last year, my son found sticker charts really motivating. There were great improvements in his behaviour. However, recently my wife and I have noticed we are on a diminishing return. How can we get extra mileage out of one of the few things that really worked?**

A *As children get older, stickers and stars start to lose their appeal. You might like to try small sums of money instead.*

9

The write stuff: improving handwriting

Many kids with ADHD have handwriting that is, frankly, shocking. Untidy, uneven letters, smudges, crossings out and splodges of correction fluid often blight imaginative work.

Even in an age when so much is written electronically, handwriting matters. Teachers can be distracted by poor presentation and mark down what would otherwise be good work.

ARE YOU SITTING COMFORTABLY?

Lots of kids have poor handwriting because they're just not sitting properly. Investing in a chair that supports the back properly can make a big difference. Also check out the height of the table. If it's too low, your child will be slouched forward; too high, and her shoulders will be tense. Neither is conducive to a neat cursive style of writing. Encourage your child to use her non-writing hand for support, and to lean on it slightly as she writes.

Here's an idea for you...

Rather than spending lots of free time slaving over handwriting exercises, construction kits or craft kits are great for developing fine motor skills. Whether it's Polish weaving, Meccano spaceships or beaded earrings, get those fingers moving and develop fine manipulation skills.

GETTING TO GRIPS

Most children with poor handwriting grip the pen or pencil too tightly, leading to achy, lazy fingers and sloppy scrawl. There's an easy way to solve this one. Buy chunky pens and pencils.

BE REALISTIC

Your child probably isn't going to win the school cup for best writing. Ever. But that's fine. Aim for legibility and clarity, not for perfection. If the pressure's off and expectations clear, writing might flow a little more easily.

SQUIGGLE TIME

Practice makes perfect, so set aside some time at the beginning or end of homework to practise squiggling. Provide some bright or glittery gel pens and coloured paper to make it fun, and ask your child to squiggle circular patterns on lined and unlined paper. Once she's perfected circles, move on to letters. Do all the anticlockwise letters on one day (a, o, c, e, s, d, g, q) and the clockwise letters the next day (r, n, m, h, k, b, p). Then do the rest.

IMPROVING CO-ORDINATION

Sometimes handwriting is a struggle because kids have a co-ordination problem. There are two types of co-ordination problems: fine motor (writing, drawing, tying shoelaces), and gross motor (running, cycling, kicking a ball).

Children with ADHD sometimes also have difficulties with fine motor co-ordination and achieving neat handwriting seems to be a particular challenge. If your child finds it hard to hit a tennis ball with a racquet, has ditched shoelaces in favour of Velcro and still has stabilisers on her bike, then poor co-ordination is likely to be the cause of her scrawly writing as well. Children who leap from one activity to the next, often tripping over toys or furniture on the way, may at first seem to have a co-ordination difficulty but actually have poor impulse control. These kids have difficulty co-ordinating their flow of movement, both when performing gross motor activities but also those fine motor activities.

Developing co-ordination won't turn a clumsy kid into Venus Williams in a weekend but, over time, you'll see improvements in all areas, including handwriting. Try ball drills. Get your child to practise throwing a netball or football into a large target, like a wheelie bin. Over time, decrease both the size of the ball and the target, so you eventually work down to ping pong balls and jam jars. Or ball

Exercise is a great way to develop co-ordination and has other great benefits for kids with ADHD. Check out IDEA 4, _Move it_, to discover more and IDEA 15, _Ritalin and other stimulant drugs_, to find out about medication which could help poor impulse control.

Try another idea...

Defining idea...

If you think you can or think you can't, you're right.
HENRY FORD

bearings and thimbles. Seriously, by the time she can throw a tennis ball into a small bucket with accuracy, her handwriting is bound to improve.

PRAISE

Children with poor handwriting typically get very demoralised. Teachers go on about it, which can be counterproductive, and progress can be slow. Judicious praise when children make or sustain an improvement can make the difference between them persevering and throwing down the pen.

Q   **My nine-year-old daughter is terribly unco-ordinated and her handwriting is just a mess. Most of the time she uses a laptop for home and schoolwork, but there are some assignments which need to be handwritten. She gets tense when she has to handwrite anything and I'm sure this doesn't help. She says she is bored of handwriting exercises and they don't seem to have made a lot of difference. Is there anything else we can try?**

How did it go?

A   *It's great that she is able to use a computer for so much of her written work. It sounds as if the only downside is that she may have lost a little confidence using a pen. You're quite right that being relaxed is sure to help. I suggest you buy her a dot-to-dot picture book. These puzzles are a good way of developing attention, pen skills and fine motor skills, as well as hand–eye co-ordination. This way she'll have a relaxed approach to developing the skills she needs and will hopefully regain some pen confidence too.*

Q   **My son's psychiatrist has suggested he sees an occupational therapist to help him with his handwriting and general clumsiness. What is an occupational therapist and how can one help?**

A   *An occupational therapist has skills and training to help your child with co-ordination. He or she will most likely have exercises to improve pen grip, organising letter formation and joining letters together. If your son is generally clumsy, he will probably also have help with tying shoelaces, throwing and catching and moving more gracefully.*

10

Say it again

Children with ADHD need to hear things and get feedback on their behaviour far more often than kids without ADHD.

So be generous with praise and compliments or, better still, letting your child know exactly what he has done well, and why you are pleased.

Any parent who has read Cinderella for the 4,507th time, ridden on the same rides at Disney World, or sat through yet another repeat of the latest cartoon will know the importance of repetition when it comes to learning. Repetition is used by all children to reinforce learning, and children with ADHD need repetition even more. Yet, as adults, we often think children with ADHD are 'getting' our ideas the first time around – but they often don't, and this is something to pay attention to and use to shape their behaviour.

A group of kindergarten teachers in the US took part in an experiment. They taught classes of children with ADHD. Each teacher was equipped with a small vibrating box with a built-in digital timer, programmed to go off at various intervals.

Here's an idea for you...

Skip long sermons. Becoming succinct will require you to learn to focus on giving feedback on things that are really important. These well-chosen words, applied frequently, have the power to change your child's behaviour.

Whenever it vibrated, the kindergarten teacher took that as her cue to give praise or other feedback to children under her care. Acting quickly and frequently improved those children's behaviour.

Research has consistently shown that children with ADHD perform better when they are given frequent feedback about their performance. So, if the behaviour you are targeting is 'listening to mummy', it is better to provide your child with feedback about how well they are listening to mummy every hour rather than doing this once at the end of the day.

There are four types of feedback to any behaviour:
- Something good can start or be presented, like praise.
- Something good can end or be taken away, like PlayStation time or an internet session.
- Something bad can start or be presented, like time out.
- Something bad can end or be taken away, like sitting alone in the classroom.

Defining idea...

The ear tends to be lazy, craves the familiar and is shocked by the unexpected; the eye, on the other hand, tends to be impatient, craves the novel and is bored by repetition.
W. H. AUDEN

Praise is an important type of feedback. Praise can include verbal praise, encouragement, attention, affection, cuddles. When you are giving praise, be honest, not gushing or overly flattering. Be specific: 'I love the way you played quietly in the kitchen while I was cooking.' But avoid giving back-handed compliments: 'I loved the way you played quietly in the kitchen. Why couldn't you have done that last night when the Joneses were here?'

Children with ADHD need to have this feedback over and over again, with much more repetition than for children without it. Kids with it seem to 'live in the moment' much more than other children, so modify their behaviour according to feedback given at that precise moment, rather than last week or yesterday. Whatever feedback you give, be it praise, cuddles or encouraging words, the more often you can give it, and give it again, the more benefit your child with ADHD will derive from it. Of course, taken to extremes, too-frequent praise will become irritating for you and your child, so mix up the types of feedback you give, perhaps alternating approval and encouragement with physical gestures like hugs. If it starts to make you feel irritated, use that as a signal to tone it down for an hour or two. Although giving more praise and using more repetition can be tiring at first, many parents are so pleased with the pay-offs in terms of behaviour that they stick with it.

Try another idea...

Learn how to give your message extra zip and zing, and ensure it falls on open ears, in IDEA 51, *Complimentary therapy.* **Teachers also need to give feedback to help children with ADHD achieve; to discover ways of working well with your child's teacher, check out IDEA 44,** *School's out.*

Defining idea...

It's the repetition of affirmations that leads to belief. And once that belief becomes a deep conviction, things begin to happen.
MUHAMMAD ALI

How did it go?

Q **Giving my daughter feedback all the time is starting to irritate my family. Often when I praise or comment, it interrupts a family activity and my husband and other children feel wound up. How can I do this in a way that doesn't feel so annoying?**

A *With many of these ideas, it's all about balance. If you do anything too often, it will inevitably feel irritating. Try to look for opportunities between activities that your child is involved in, so that you are not perceived as intrusive. The actual time interval is something to experiment with; the important point is that a child with ADHD needs frequent feedback.*

Q **I get tired giving compliments endlessly, especially as they don't always feel deserved. There are so many times when I wish I could let my son know how I really feel. I get so drained. Can you help?**

A *It is tiring to give compliments so much of the time. Giving regular feedback isn't just about giving praise. You can give negative feedback too, and be just as prompt at giving consequences for misdemeanours. Giving praise is a great way to increase your child's desire to please you and increase the amount of positive feelings between you and your child. Being clear and specific, and doing this often, will help your child develop positive behaviour in the long run, and ultimately make his behaviour less challenging.*

11

Brothers and sisters

ADHD is a family affair. One child may have the diagnosis but, more often than not, brothers and sisters also suffer. There are things families can do to lessen the impact.

One family sent their other children to boarding school, but you don't need to go down the Hogwarts route or wait until your other children are putting themselves up for adoption.

BROKEN TOYS

Children with ADHD are impulsive, sometimes forget what is theirs and their poor fine motor skills and poor co-ordination can make them rough and inquisitive with other people's toys. It really is heartbreaking when kids with ADHD are reckless or clumsy with their siblings' toys and accidentally damage or break them. Non-negotiable rules about toy ownership are the best way forward. Do all you can to protect your other children's belongings, providing locks to toy chests, declaring no-go zones and being clear about who is allowed to touch what, when and where. You might like to consider allowing older siblings to have locks on their doors.

Here's an idea for you...

Children with ADHD are often messy and disorganised. If you can, give them their own room, even if other siblings need to share. There will be fewer squabbles and dramas in the long run. If you don't have space for a separate room, mark off an area that belongs to each child using tape and provide everyone sharing with lockable storage. Set aside a homework area that is not in a shared bedroom to avoid any interruptions.

TIME DIFFERENCE

Many children who have a brother or sister with ADHD feel resentful of the disproportionate amount of parental time that their sibling gets. At best, you'll hear them grumble about it. At worst they'll act out and may even start copying some ADHD behaviour to claw back some of your time. Children with ADHD do take up an inordinate amount of time and energy, but it doesn't all have to be yours. When you are planning your week, think about how the amount of time you are going to spend with each child could be more equal. Could grandma take your ADHD child to his medication review appointment, and dad supervise homework one evening while you take the others swimming? It requires a bit of thought, but recruiting other adult helpers is well worth the effort.

DIFFERENT CHILDREN, SAME RULES

Many parents are more lenient towards their child with ADHD than towards their healthier siblings. This causes no end of resentment and guarantees a regular chorus of 'that's not fair, mum'. The hard fact is that children with ADHD are different and do require a different approach sometimes. A child who is not by nature impulsive may require a firmer reprimand than an impulsive kid who has had a lapse.

The trick to managing this is clarity. Explain to the other children in your household what ADHD means. If they know upfront that their quirky brother can't always help himself, and that this is why there are sometimes different rules, it makes their perceived unfairness that bit more palatable.

Consistency is key to successful ADHD management. Check out IDEA 12, *Home uniform*, to understand how to achieve an unswerving parenting style in different settings.

Try another idea...

Children with ADHD will often butt in when their siblings have playmates over or are involved in a game. Friends get fed up and may stop coming unless you take remedial action. ADHD kids often struggle socially, so are less likely to have their own friends over at the same time. To minimise the risks of your son sabotaging his brothers' and sisters' friendships, set some rules about what you do and don't expect to see him doing. Provide a structured activity for him to do and spend some time playing with him while his siblings have friends visiting. Provide heaps of praise when he plays co-operatively or is invited to join in with their games.

Even though there will be times when your place feels more like a war zone than a family home, bear in mind that most brothers and sisters do eventually work things out for themselves, making adaptations for their sibling with ADHD and learning how to stay out of the way of tantrums and missiles.

Joint undertakings stand a better chance when they benefit both sides.
EURIPIDES

Defining idea...

47

How did it go?

Q **A family we know has a system where if one child breaks another's toy, it has to be replaced using the culprit's pocket money. Would this be a fair system to use in our household where my son with ADHD often ends up breaking his sister's rather delicate doll's house accessories?**

A *Quite a few families do this, and often damaged toys end up being replaced by a sort of direct debit system from the culprit's pocket money. I think this should only happen if there is wilful rather than accidental damage, as otherwise children with ADHD are effectively being penalised for having a disability. I'd suggest more secure measures for your daughter's delicate toys and stricter rules about your son touching them.*

Q **My son has ADHD and family outings often come to an abrupt finish because of his behaviour. We frequently just can't manage in places like zoos and theme parks and our other three children complain that it isn't fair on them. What can we do?**

A *They're right, it isn't fair. You can't make it any fairer for them when activities are cut short, but you can make it up to them. Instead of trying to do things as a whole family, why not do things in smaller family groups with one parent in each group? That way you can do things with them that would be much tougher if your son was there.*

12

Home uniform

Impulsive children struggle to plan ahead. Timetables, predictable schedules and consistency in the face of misbehaviour are key to living happily with ADHD.

Time invested in developing routines for your ADHD child will pay sizeable dividends. Standard, unsurprising schedules help children who find it difficult to organise, plan and remember.

GETTING READY

A little groundwork is essential before introducing consistency into your child's life. Set aside some planning time with your partner on quiet nights (after the children are in bed) when there are no distractions. It can be a good idea to plan daily routines, determine what each of your children will be doing. Are there any after-school activities, for instance?

Here's an
idea for
you...

Parents do things differently, that's a given. Even if you live and parent together, one of you is likely to be more lenient or to be quicker to praise. So your child has learnt to play parents off against each other? Try using 'first past the post'. The first parent to notice a broken rule or other misbehaviour intervenes in his or her preferred way, no questions asked.

LIKE CLOCKWORK

Once you've spent this time planning, you'll be ready to plot out your child's daily routines. You might also like to think about whether you will implement giving rewards for sticking to these routines. Young children with ADHD often struggle to get organised for school in the morning, so you could introduce a small reward, like a treat for their lunchbox, if they are ready on time.

Give your child a copy of his daily routine, and put it somewhere he can see it, such as in his bedroom or on the fridge. If you have more than one child, and are using this idea with all of them, it's important that each has their own personalised routine, and not a shared one, even if they have some activities in common.

BE SPECIFIC

These schedules only work if children know what is expected of them. Kids with ADHD need explicit instructions and prompts. So instead of writing 'get ready for school', for example, you need to write a checklist. It might look like this:

- Out of bed
- Clean teeth
- Shower
- Get dressed in school uniform
- Check homework is in schoolbag

- Eat breakfast
- Collect packed lunch
- Be at bus stop by 7.40 a.m.

Don't forget to include activities like household chores.

Children who love routines often find transitions difficult. IDEA 3, *Flexible friends*, will help prepare them.

Try another idea...

GET ORGANISED

Set up your child's bedroom so that each toy and item of clothing has a clear place. You might like to make labels or other visual cues for these places. An excess of toys can be overwhelming and cause minds to flit from one activity to another, like a butterfly. If you suspect you have too many toys at home, why not pack a few away into boxes and rotate them every couple of months?

CONTINGENCIES

Setting consistent rules and limits helps children feel safe. A big part of getting consistent is planning for misbehaviours. Children with ADHD are more likely to act on impulse and do things like throwing a cricket ball inside. The best time to make contingencies is not when the window is broken but at a quiet time while nothing untoward is happening. Imagine every worst-case scenario and decide what the consequence for each should be. Now the hard part. You need to reach some sort of consensus with your child's other parent and anyone else who looks after him.

Defining idea...

What matters to children is the way in which you present your differences, rather than the fact you have conflicting views.
ANDREA CLIFFORD-POSTON, child, family and educational therapist

Think of as much misbehaviour as you can and come up with a plan. At a time when your child is not misbehaving explain what the consequences for common misbehaviours will be, so that he knows exactly what to expect. Try not to go overboard when you explain this, or he'll feel told off. Just use your best business-like voice, explain, and move on to a different topic once the message has gone in. Share your contingency plans with the other adults who look after him. This way, when any adult caregiver finds your child misbehaving, they will know exactly what to do and your child will have completely consistent discipline.

Q **Consistency is easier said than done. We tried to ensure that our seven year old eats his main meal before pudding, but unfortunately anything goes at school meals and he often eats pudding first. I know teachers have other children to look after but can you suggest a way we might achieve some consistency?**

A *First of all, please relax. It's great that he's eating. Many children with ADHD lose concentration during meals and wander off, or have reduced appetites if they are taking stimulant medication. One idea might be to agree some key rules, and communicate these to his class teacher.*

Q **I have a very creative and impulsive little boy who is also creative in his misdemeanours. Neither his teacher, his father nor I foresaw any of these challenges and so didn't have a plan for them. How can we make sure we are unified in our approach, when he is so haphazard in his?**

A *You've made a really good point. No parent is going to be able to accurately predict every mischief. Children with ADHD have a lot of energy and their impulsiveness means they will often come up with new things to try. Next time he misbehaves in a way that is unpredictable, find something comparable on your list of predictable misbehaviours and discipline according to that. Let his teacher and father know at the next opportunity so you are all working together. The most important thing is that your child understands that whatever he does, both you and other adults in his life will back each other up.*

How did it go?

53

13

Giving children choices

Children enjoy choices. Just like adults, they appreciate having some say in what goes on in their lives.

It doesn't come much simpler than this. Let children make some decisions for themselves, and they will learn good judgement and to accept responsibility.

Giving children with ADHD chances to make choices is an essential part of managing their behaviour problems. Most parents want to encourage their offspring to think for themselves and come up with their own ideas, but parents of children with ADHD can sometimes lose confidence in their kids' ability to do this. Show children you believe that they can make good choices, and their self-esteem will soar. Kids with ADHD often feel out of control. Being allowed to make choices helps them feel much more in control.

The benefits of giving children choice are many. Here are some you should notice:
- Greater levels of co-operation.
- Better self-discipline.
- An improvement in decision-making skills.

Work simple choices into your child's routine today. Start with just one or two. Let her select which choice she wants and then go along with it. Here are some choices you could give:

- **Do you want to clean your teeth first or put on your pyjamas?**
- **Which chore would you like to do: unloading the dishwasher or emptying the bins?**
- **Do you want to wear your black shoes or your brown ones?**
- **Do you want to do all your homework on Sunday evening or spread it through the weekend?**

- A sense of self-control.
- An increase in confidence.
- Thinking more before acting impulsively.

Parents of children with ADHD are often understandably wary of offering too many choices, resorting instead to a stream of commands. Like other parents, you may find yourself relying on logic or gut feeling to keep your child safe, and make the decisions. It feels natural to give clear instructions rather than options, especially after children have made some unwise choices. However, this can be counterproductive. If children with ADHD are not given opportunities to consider their options, make conscientious choices and learn from mistakes, the results could be disastrous once they are faced with the need to make potentially more serious decisions as a teenager.

Grab any opportunity to give children choices. Even very young children can be given the choice of which book they would like read to them, which snack they would like to have or which toy they would like to play with. These decisions may seem simple, but even these choices begin to teach a child important life lessons, like patience, consequences and compromise.

The language you use when offering choices is critical. Often, children are asked if they want to do something when they really have no actual choice. Consider this: avoid asking yes or no questions unless you're willing to accept no as an answer, and ask your child which book she would like to read, rather than whether or not she would like to read a book.

Once again, this idea works best in combination. Children with good problem-solving skills will be better equipped to think creatively about choices. Try developing those skills by turning to IDEA 39, *Problem solving*.

Try another idea...

Children take us seriously when we offer them choices. Children with ADHD can become frustrated very quickly if they are not able to do what they want. The most important thing is that choice is kept realistic. Most difficulties arise when parents offer choices they don't really mean, so only offer children choices when all of the options are realistic and safe.

Offer options that you would be equally comfortable for your child to take, and which are clear and possible. For example, if you say 'sit still at the table or go to your room' and your daughter then goes to her room, only for you to shout, 'come back here until you've learnt to sit still at the table', you're not being fair. After all, she did one of the things you asked her to do.

"It is our choices that show what we truly are, far more than our abilities."
J. K. ROWLING, Professor Dumbledore to Harry Potter

Defining idea...

How did it go?

Q **There seem to be so many things my daughter has to do, it's hard to see how to offer more choices. Could you give some advice on how to offer choices around things which are pretty non-negotiable, like taking medication?**

A *While taking medicine is itself non-negotiable, offering simple choices gives your daughter a needed sense of control. You might ask, 'Do you want the medicine before you get dressed or afterwards?'*

Q **My son has ADHD and a mild learning disability. He isn't able to make sensible choices so I have to choose for him. I find it hard to believe that he will ever make good choices. For instance, he might choose to neglect his homework or wear a T-shirt when the weather is cold and not take a sweater. If he chose his own lunch, he would choose just sweets and crisps. What can I do?**

A *Sounds like it's time to take a risk and relinquish some control. Take his lunchbox as an example. If he fills it with sweets one day, it's no huge deal in the wider scheme of things. Better still, offer some guidance. Asking questions like, 'would you like to take an apple or some grapes?' rather than giving him free rein enables him to make some safely guided choices. It sounds harsh, but the most important choice is one you are facing: let him develop and learn or keep wrapping him in cotton wool.*

14

Atomoxetine

If your child has reacted badly to a stimulant drug, or not reacted at all, don't despair. There are other drugs that may help, and one of them is atomoxetine.

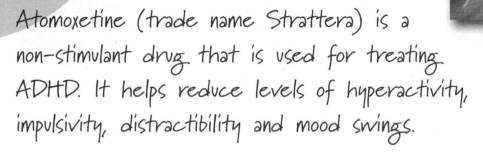

Atomoxetine (trade name Strattera) is a non-stimulant drug that is used for treating ADHD. It helps reduce levels of hyperactivity, impulsivity, distractibility and mood swings.

Atomoxetine is manufactured and marketed under the trade name Strattera by Eli Lilly and as Attentin by Torrent Pharmaceuticals. It was originally developed as an antidepressant drug. In scientific trials, no antidepressant effects were found, but it was later found to be helpful in ADHD.

Atomoxetine works by blocking or slowing noradrenaline reabsorption in the brain. This means that it strengthens the chemical signal between those nerves that use noradrenaline to send messages. Noradrenaline is a chemical messenger that has an important role in regulating attention, impulsivity and activity levels. It also

Here's an idea for you...

If your child feels jumpy or irritable taking stimulants, atomoxetine may be worth trying. Alternatively, if your child has been taking stimulant drugs and has not seen good benefits, why not speak to a specialist about atomoxetine?

increases levels of dopamine, which is thought to be lower than normal in children with ADHD. Atomoxetine works on those parts of the brain that control attention, impulsivity and activity.

Children taking atomoxetine should be less restless, more able to concentrate and more likely to think about something before they do it. However, studies to date haven't looked at whether atomoxetine still works if it's taken for longer than a few weeks.

Children taking atomoxetine:

- **Concentrate more.** Your child may find it easier to concentrate, to follow instructions and to focus on things such as homework, and may also be less likely to forget or lose things. Also, schoolwork may improve.
- **Feel less overactive.** If your child is always on the go, he or she may feel calmer and less restless after taking atomoxetine, may be more likely to sit still and less likely to run about and fidget.
- **Are less impulsive.** Your child may find it easier to think before acting, to wait his or her turn and to resist interrupting other people's conversations. Your child may be less likely to blurt out answers before questions have been finished, and may become less argumentative.
- **Are less disruptive.** This can help reduce strain at home and at school, which may help your child cope better with day-to-day activities.

Continuing to take atomoxetine can also reduce the chances that your child's symptoms of ADHD will come back.

Atomoxetine needs to be given once or twice every day. Most children will take a daily dose but others have this divided into morning and early evening doses. Whereas stimulant drugs like methylphenidate work almost instantly, it may take a week or so before you notice any

Stimulant drugs are usually the drug treatment of choice for ADHD. Find out all about them in IDEA 15, *Ritalin and other stimulant drugs.*

Try another idea...

improvements. If your child has previously taken a stimulant drug, you are likely to notice quickly that there are no immediate effects with atomoxetine and that can seem a bit strange. Most children will be started on a very low dose, and if they show signs of improvement on that low dose, it will gradually be increased until the best possible response occurs. Children get used to atomoxetine over a period of weeks, and usually most effects are noticed after a month of taking it. Some parents and children have noticed benefits of atomoxetine as early as the end of the first week.

SIDE EFFECTS

Unfortunately, no drug is free of side effects. The most common side effect here is decreased appetite. Other common side effects include tiredness, an upset stomach, nausea and vomiting, sleep disturbance, dizziness, a dry mouth and mood swings. Atomoxetine has other rare but serious side effects, including liver damage. Contact your child's specialist if he or she has a racing heart beat, feels very sick or drowsy or has yellowed skin or eye whites.

A child deserves the maximum respect.
HORACE

Defining idea...

A review of recent studies has shown that a small number of children and young people who take atomoxetine are more likely to think about killing themselves. In September 2005, atomoxetine was found to increase the risk of suicidal thoughts among children and adolescents. One attempted suicide and five instances of suicidal thoughts were reported out of 1,357 young patients taking Strattera, while none were reported out of a control group of 851 taking placebos. So, if your child is taking atomoxetine, your doctor will most likely recommend that you watch closely for changes in mood or behaviour, and immediately contact the specialist if you notice anything untoward. Atomoxetine can cause fits in some people. For this reason, doctors are cautious about prescribing it for children who have had fits before.

Q **Is there any difference in how effective the drug is when it is given once a day compared to when the dose is split between morning and evening?**

A *Research suggests that atomoxetine works as well when given in one dose in the morning as it does when the dose is split in two.*

Q **Is there a lower age limit for atomoxetine? My five-year-old daughter has ADHD and her doctor has said she is not able to have stimulant medication as she is too young. Might she be able to have atomoxetine instead?**

A *All the scientific trials that have been done so far have looked at children aged between six and twelve. We know that atomoxetine works well with them, and is safe in this age group. There isn't enough evidence of it working well and safely in younger children and more research is needed before it can be recommended for little ones like your daughter. In fact it is only approved to be used in children between the ages of six and twelve.*

How did it go?

63

15

Ritalin and other stimulant drugs

They may not be a universal panacea, but it's worth sorting facts from fiction when it comes to Ritalin and the other stimulants.

OK, it looks slightly strange giving stimulant drugs to children who seem hyperstimulated already. But there's good reason for this — and a lot of the time, it works wonders.

When it comes to stimulant drugs, people tend to fall into one of two camps. There are the enthusiasts, who will ask for a prescription before a diagnosis has even been made, and then there are the devout sceptics, who see stimulants as being bad and unnatural. If you're in the latter group, you could – of course – skip this part, but I'd like to make a plea for you to read through to the end. You don't have to wholeheartedly agree with every word, but you might find something of interest.

Stimulant medication can improve attention span, decrease distractibility, increase ability to finish tasks, decrease hyperactivity and improve your child's ability to think before doing. Many parents find their child's homework and schoolwork improve when they are taking these drugs, too. It might seem paradoxical, but

Here's an idea for you...

If your child is given a prescription for stimulant medication, give the first dose on a weekend morning so you can see what the effects are. These drugs act quickly, so you will see any beneficial effects or side effects quickly. You can then let teachers know what to expect, too.

although stimulant drugs stimulate the central nervous system, they have a calming effect on children with ADHD. These drugs work by increasing dopamine, a neurotransmitter which is important for attention and focus.

There are a number of commonly used stimulant drugs, including:

- Methylphenidate (Ritalin, Concerta, Metadate, Daytrana)
- Dexamfetamine (Dexedrine, Dextrostat)
- Adderall (mixed salts of amphetamines)

There are different formulations of stimulant drugs, which mostly affect their duration of action. Short-acting stimulants last between three and five hours. Longer-acting ones last up to twelve hours. All short-acting drugs need to be taken several times a day, including during school hours. As the drug wears off, rebound effects are common, and symptoms can increase. This is why long-acting formulations tend to be preferred by both prescribers and parents. Because all these drugs can affect appetite, it makes sense to give them after a meal or snack. When they wear off towards the end of the day, many children experience rebound effects of restlessness. Your doctor can help you get round this by using the smallest dose possible in the late afternoon.

SIDE EFFECTS

All drugs do, unfortunately, have some side effects, and stimulant drugs are no exception. The common side effects listed below usually don't last any longer than two weeks. If they persist, or if your child has other effects than these, speak to your specialist:

- Loss of appetite
- Trouble falling asleep
- Tummy aches and upsets
- Headaches
- Feeling sad or crying easily
- Being more cranky or irritable than usual

Stimulant medication works best when it is used in combination with other non-drug interventions for ADHD. Check out IDEA 8, *Stars and stickers*, to get started. IDEA 20, *Drug holidays*, explains the merits of planned breaks.

Try another idea...

If your child develops any new movements, tics or twitches, they should be reported to your specialist at once. Likewise, sad feelings that last more than a few days must be brought to medical attention.

GETTING HOOKED

Lots of parents worry that giving children stimulant drugs may make them addicted or even more likely to abuse illegal drugs in future. However, studies indicate that the opposite is true. These drugs lack the key properties that create addiction, particularly in the doses used for treating ADHD. Although methylphenidates have properties similar to amphetamines, their drug levels rise very slowly in the brain at the oral doses given for ADHD. This slow rise prevents a 'high' and addiction.

In fact, methylphenidate might even protect young people with ADHD from abusing alcohol, nicotine or other drugs because it can reduce the need to self-medicate ADHD symptoms using these 'alternatives'. That means they may be less likely to experiment than would otherwise be the case.

I was trying to daydream, but my mind kept wandering.
STEVE WRIGHT, comedian

Defining idea...

How did it go?

Q   My son is taking methylphenidate and it has really helped him. He also gets bad hay fever but has been told he can't take hay-fever medication as it interacts. Is there another type of drug for ADHD that he could take?

A   *If methylphenidate is working so well, it makes sense for him to continue taking it if at all possible. Children taking stimulant drugs often become more hyperactive when they take antihistamines for allergies. There are some drugs for hay fever that do not cross the blood–brain barrier. This means they act on hay fever symptoms but do not act on the brain, so they are much better for children with ADHD. You might like to speak to your doctor about using these antihistamines instead, rather than finding another drug for his ADHD.*

Q   My wife wants our son to try taking methylphenidate but I'm worried about him being doped up. Won't it make him behave like a zombie?

A   *I can understand why you are worried – many people think along these lines – but the short answer is no. These stimulant drugs turn on parts of the brain that are believed to be underactive in kids with hyperactivity and are not sedating or soothing in the way that tranquillisers are. Other people may well notice a difference if he is on medication, as his behaviour is likely to improve, but they are very unlikely to notice any 'zombieness'.*

16

Ten principles for fine-tuning stimulant medication

Most children who take stimulant medication enjoy improvements. It can take a little fine-tuning to get the dose right.

Parents, children and professionals need to work as a tight team to make sure children are on the lowest effective dose of stimulants. These principles help you do that.

The vast majority of children with ADHD experience an improvement in symptoms when taking stimulant medication. When a trial of stimulants fails or is less than successful, it often makes sense to review dosing strategies and check that these are optimised. Doctors often find it difficult to predict which dose will give the best results. For each child, doses are tailored according to their size and age and also to their responses to medication. This bespoke approach requires a bit of trial and error, which can be frustrating for parents and teachers, but your role in observation is hugely important. The better you can understand the following dosing principles, the better placed you will be to work in a team with your child's specialist and find the right dose.

Here's an idea for you...

If your child is taking medicines at different times during the day, ask a pharmacist for a morning, afternoon and night pill dispenser and load this up in the evenings when you make school lunches. These dispensers contain small boxes that allow you to store tablets for the correct time of day and make it easy to see if a dose is due or has been missed.

1. Before starting new medication or changing a dose, parents and professionals need to have absolute clarity about which specific behaviours you are expecting the medication to alter. Misunderstandings about what is being treated are common. Stimulant drugs affect the attention and behaviour problems that are part of ADHD. They won't cure naughtiness, wilfulness or hostility. Children will be able to concentrate better but they won't turn a slow learner into a mini Einstein.

2. Everyone's goal is to use the lowest possible dosage that produces improved behaviour.

3. If there is no obvious change in behaviour two hours after giving a stimulant drug, it hasn't worked. A dose increase or different medication are needed.

4. Regular and frequent follow-up appointments will be necessary after changing a dose to monitor response and to detect possible side effects. Gradual, cautious changes are more likely to be successful. Once medication is fine-tuned and the correct dose has been established, follow up can be much more infrequent.

5. If the effects of stimulant medication seem to wear off at homework time, an increase in the mid-afternoon dose usually does the trick.

6. When children are especially challenging first thing, or have difficulty travelling to school because of ADHD symptoms, a dose on waking is worth trying.

7. Be alert to side effects after any dose increase. Almost all side effects happen at the beginning of treatment or when there is a dose hike. If your child is suddenly tearful or irritable for no reason, stimulant medication needs to be stopped.

8. If children's ADHD affects them in the classroom, causing difficulty with learning, but does not interfere too much with home life or play, they may only need medication on school days and can skip doses at weekends.

9. If an initial regimen doesn't work, changing the dose, adding another drug or changing to a different medication often brings improvement. If children don't respond to standard doses of stimulant medication, it doesn't make sense to try higher doses. Changing to a different drug is preferable. On the other hand, if there has been a partial improvement, a dose increase rather than a new drug is a good idea. Some experts recommend trying a second stimulant if a first one fails. If the child still doesn't respond, atomoxetine, clonidine or antidepressants may be beneficial.

10. Involve your child in all dose changes. Ask him what he notices. It might be that he gets into trouble less at school or that more people want to play with him.

If stimulants cause tics, or if your child already has a tic disorder, doctors may suggest clonidine. Find out all about it in IDEA 18, *Clonidine*.

Try another idea…

A hundred objective measurements didn't sum up the worth of a garden; only the delight of its users did that. Only the use made it mean something.
LOIS MCMASTER BUJOLD, *A Civil Campaign*

Defining idea…

71

How did it go?

Q **My son has ADHD and is on Ritalin. It helps a lot during the day, but at night he finds it really hard to get to sleep, saying his mind is racing. His usual doctor cut out his after-school dose, which made homework time hellish. When we went back to the doctor we saw a locum who suggested he might need an extra dose before bedtime. This sounds like the opposite advice, and we're not sure what to do. What do you suggest?**

A *Although it sounds contradictory, there's logic in both suggestions. For most children, it makes sense to cut an afternoon dose if they have difficulty sleeping as a result of the stimulant drug. For a minority, though, a late evening dose of stimulant medication stops the mind racing and paradoxically helps them sleep. There's no way of knowing if your son is in this minority, so I would suggest speaking again to your regular specialist and considering trying an evening dose on a holiday or weekend night.*

Q **I misunderstood the doctor's instructions and accidentally gave my son twice the prescribed amount of Ritalin. How will this double dose affect him?**

A *The greatest effect will probably be on your nerves. Things like this do happen and can be incredibly perturbing for parents. Stimulant drugs are safe, even at an accidentally higher dose. He might be subdued or withdrawn and have trouble settling to sleep, but there probably won't be anything more sinister than that.*

17

Antidepressants: sad, bad or dangerous to know?

When stimulant medication is ineffective, other drugs are considered. Antidepressants are sometimes used as an alternative for treating ADHD.

Some older antidepressant drugs have been found to have some effects on ADHD. Newer antidepressants do not have an effect on impulsivity or inattention, though.

Although some antidepressants can help with symptoms of ADHD, they are less effective than stimulants and so are not used as first-line drug treatment. Hyperactivity improves with certain antidepressants, and there are also some beneficial effects on impulsivity, and a minimal effect on attention. Because of the side effects of these drugs, they are usually the third or fourth choice of drug. Doctors therefore refer to them as the 'third or fourth line'.

TRICYCLIC ANTIDEPRESSANTS (DESIPRAMINE, IMIPRAMINE)

The group of antidepressants known as tricyclics has been prescribed for children whose symptoms do not get better with stimulants or who also have tics, anxiety or

Here's an idea for you...

If your child has been taking antidepressants for some time, and if you're unsure if they're still having an effect, speak to your doctor about having a trial off medication. This is the only way to know if they are still making a difference. Ask for Connor's questionnaires (used to assess ADHD) for yourself, your child and the school to complete when your child is not on medication so your doctor can compare these results with those he scored when he was on medication.

depression. Parents typically notice some improvement within a few hours of the first dose, but the effect is much less dramatic than with stimulant medication. Greater benefits are noticeable after a couple of days, however, and about a fortnight after starting treatment, the best effects are seen.

The most common side effect is sedation and sleepiness, making some children feel hung over, but tricyclics have other side effects, including having a dry mouth, blurred vision and constipation. However, these side effects are much more common in adults taking tricyclic drugs for depression than they are in children; much smaller doses are used when treating kids with ADHD. They have fallen out of favour in recent years as they can have serious side effects including effects on the heart and are very toxic in overdose. Some specialists still recommend tricyclics when stimulant medication doesn't work or can't be used for medical reasons. In the past specialists opted for tricyclics when a child with ADHD had Tourette's syndrome or other tics. Now it is much more common for clonidine to be used in combination with a stimulant drug for children who have a tic disorder as well as ADHD.

SSRIs

The antidepressant family known as selective serotonin reuptake inhibitors (SSRIs) includes fluoxetine (Prozac), sertraline, citalopram and paroxetine. SSRIs are sometimes used when specialists are treating children who have depression as well as ADHD. However, their effects on core ADHD symptoms are minimal and they could even make things worse as they might worsen impulsivity. The only SSRI that should be used to treat depression in children and teenagers is fluoxetine (Prozac) as the others have not been shown to be beneficial and have been linked to an increase in suicidal feelings.

Antidepressants are never the first choice of drug treatment for ADHD. Check out IDEA 15, *Ritalin and other stimulant drugs*, to find out about the most likely option. Children with other conditions as well need different types of treatment – see IDEA 30, *Double whammy*.

Try another idea...

SELEGILINE

This is an old-fashioned antidepressant which is broken down by the body into compounds found in methamphetamine (a stimulant). It blocks monoamine oxidase B, an enzyme that breaks down dopamine. It hasn't been widely studied in children with ADHD but research indicates it may be effective at improving some symptoms in children who have ADHD, even if they are not depressed as well.

Trust one who has gone through it.
VIRGIL

Defining idea...

VENLAFAXINE (TRADE NAME EFFEXOR)

Venlafaxine targets neurotransmitters that are not targeted by older antidepressants. It may be particularly helpful for treating patients with ADHD and some accompanying disorders, including depression or conduct disorder. Venlafaxine can be highly poisonous in overdose, especially if it is mixed with other drugs and alcohol, so it may well not be top of your specialist's list if you're the parent of an impulsive teen with mood swings and impulsivity.

75

How did it go?

Q My sister, who is a nurse, told me that tricyclic antidepressants are as effective as stimulant drugs but are not addictive. Is she right?

A *There are two issues here. Your sister is correct in saying that tricyclic antidepressants are not addictive. But neither are stimulant drugs. There was one good-quality scientific trial carried out in the US that indicated imipramine, one of the tricyclic antidepressants, was just as effective as stimulant medication. However, the findings from this study have not been replicated or borne out in widespread clinical practice. Because of the potentially risky side-effect profile of tricyclic antidepressants, and the relative safety of stimulants, it is sound clinical practice to use stimulant drugs as a first choice.*

Q My son's specialist has recently suggested trying imipramine, but I've heard that children can become used to it and that the dose will need to be repeatedly increased. I'm not happy with the idea that the amount might need to be cranked up and up. Is what I've been told true?

A *Some children do become tolerant to imipramine, and parents and doctors notice this when improvements in behaviour and attention are not maintained. Clinical practice suggests that one dose increase may be useful, but if children become tolerant to the increased dose, a change of medication is better than repeated increases, with their inherent side effects.*

18

Clonidine

If your child's ADHD is raising your blood pressure, an antihypertensive drug may just be the answer. But it's not for you...

A drug originally developed for treating high blood pressure also has beneficial effects on impulsivity and aggression. It isn't suitable for everyone, but might work for your child.

Yes, clonidine was originally developed as a treatment for hypertension but it is also effective in treating ADHD. It works by stimulating brain receptors which in turn causes blood vessels in certain parts of the body to relax. Another effect of clonidine is that it inhibits the production of noradrenaline in the brain and this is thought to be important in hyperactivity. Experts think that ADHD could be partly due to an imbalance of chemicals in the front part of the brain. It's this part of the brain that controls how you move and feel. By stopping the brain making noradrenaline, clonidine may improve the balance of chemicals and improve symptoms. It has also been used to treat Tourette's syndrome by reducing tics, improving hyperactivity and decreasing obsessive-compulsive symptoms.

Here's an idea for you...

Clonidine patches – which can be worn like a plaster – can be useful if you need to get round problems associated with taking medication at school. Children can have a bath or swim with a patch on, but it does need to be changed every five days.

Clonidine is not commonly used as a treatment for ADHD everywhere, though a specialist may prescribe it if your child's behaviour does not improve with a stimulant like methylphenidate. Clonidine is useful as a treatment for ADHD because it can have a beneficial effect on impulsivity and oppositional behaviour. It is more effective in controlling aggressive and hyperaroused symptoms than other drugs. However, it improves inattentive symptoms to a lesser extent than other drugs do. It is also good at reducing tics so is useful for children who have tics as well as hyperactivity. Put simply, clonidine may be helpful for your child if she is predominantly impulsive and fidgety or squirmy, but not if she is more distractible with a short attention span. If she leaves her seat a lot in class, or runs about and climbs excessively, clonidine may be helpful.

Clonidine is sometimes used together with stimulant drugs like methylphenidate (Ritalin) to treat ADHD. Methylphenidate helps learning and attentiveness. This combination, which enables specific treatment of attention with one drug and activity with another, is often worth investigating. Some parents have been alarmed by reports, which are widely reported on some websites, that there were four sudden deaths in the 1980s linked to the combination of clonidine and methylphenidate. These deaths were investigated and it was concluded that they were not due to combination treatment. Review of each of the four tragic cases demonstrated other causes of death, including a problem with a coronary artery, postnatal cardiac damage and a grand-mal seizure.

SIDE EFFECTS

The major downside of clonidine is that it tends to make kids sleepy. For this reason, clonidine is started at bedtime. If a child with ADHD is having trouble sleeping, this side effect can work to your advantage. As it was developed as a treatment for blood pressure, it will be no surprise that it can also significantly lower blood pressure. For this reason, clonidine must be started at a low dose, which is increased gradually and cautiously, until an effective and safe dosage level is reached. Missing doses can cause rapid heartbeats and other symptoms that may lead to severe problems. Other common side effects include constipation, dizziness, dry eyes and sometimes blurred vision, and a dry mouth. The less common side effects are headache, anxiety and skin rashes.

One small study involving twenty-four boys found that some children given clonidine (either alone or with methylphenidate) had a higher risk of developing a slow heart rhythm. For this reason it makes sense to have your child's pulse and blood pressure checked at each appointment with the specialist.

Unlike stimulant drugs which work immediately, clonidine takes time to have an effect. It may take four to five weeks before improvements in impulsivity and hyperactivity are seen. Clonidine is available as tablets or as a skin patch which can be useful for children who have difficulty swallowing pills (or who are unable to do so).

Try another idea...

Clonidine is often used in conjunction with methylphenidate. Check out IDEA 15, *Ritalin and other stimulant drugs*, to find out more about it.

Defining idea...

To have begun is half the job; be bold and be sensible.
HORACE

How did it go?

Q My son made good progress on clonidine. However he gets a very dry mouth and I'm not sure how to help him. In summer it is really unbearable and he doesn't want to take his medication. What do you suggest?

A *Sucking on sugar-free boiled sweets can help. In summer you could also try giving him ice lollies to suck, or offer regular chewing gum. Make sure he has access to water all the time. If none of these suggestions work, and he's still feeling uncomfortable, talk to your doctor about a saliva substitute. This is a medical way of relieving a dry mouth and may just do the trick.*

Q My daughter has Tourette's and ADHD and clonidine has helped her. A recent dose increase has improved her tics and impulsivity but made her very sleepy. Is there a way of making her less sleepy without changing the dose, or do we just have to put up with it?

A *It's so frustrating when, after a lot of fine-tuning, a dose is effective at eliminating troublesome symptoms but the price is a new or worsened side effect. Sleepiness can sometimes be reduced by giving clonidine in small, frequent doses and this might be something you'd like to speak to her specialist about.*

19

A fat lot of good

The right nutrients can help children (and their parents) think faster, be better co-ordinated and balanced, and have improved concentration.

Omega 3 has been centre stage in many healthy eating campaigns, and with good reason.

By putting the right food on your family table and in your children's lunchboxes, you could help with hyperactivity and also boost intelligence, improve mood, help them be more emotionally stable, sharpen memories and keep their minds active. Several scientific studies have shown promising results by using omega-3 fatty acids for improvements in behaviour of children with ADHD. Larger trials are needed to confirm these findings, and to establish whether there are long-lasting benefits, as well as optimal formulations and dosages. That said, omega-3 fatty acids clearly play a key role in brain-cell development and certainly seem to alleviate symptoms in some children with ADHD.

Omega 3 is called an essential fatty acid because our bodies need it but we cannot produce it ourselves. Essential fatty acids are needed for several body systems, including the cardiovascular and nervous systems. Almost half the fat from which the brain is built is made up of one of the omega-3 acids called docosahexaenoic acid (DHA). The two other major dietary omega-3 acids are alpha-linolenic acid (ALA) and eicosapentaenoic acid (EPA).

Here's an idea for you...

Aiming to include a source of omega 3 into meals every day? Serving fish and seafood such as salmon, halibut, tuna and scallops a few times a week is an easy way to increase your child's omega-3 intake. You needn't start from scratch at every meal. Open a can of salmon, empty it into a blender with some cream cheese and a squirt of lemon, whizz them together and spread it on toast or use it as a dip.

Defining idea...

Many people really aren't aware of the sheer importance of food and diet for the brain. Omega 3s can improve brain function at the very simplest level, by improving blood flow.
DR ALEX RICHARDSON, senior research fellow in physiology at Mansfield College, University of Oxford

In one study, children taking omega-3 fatty acid supplements were assessed. This particular study followed an experimental method called a randomised double-blind controlled trial. Half the children were given omega-3 fatty acids and half were given placebos. Neither the children nor those evaluating their progress knew which group was taking which treatment. The ones taking the omega 3 had significant improvements in behaviour, reading and spelling. In another trial, researchers studied boys with behavioural difficulties and learning problems, and found that those with lower omega-3 levels had more behaviour problems and temper tantrums, and more sleep difficulties.

And in Australia, laboratory rats deprived of essential fatty acids including omega 3 at particular developmental stages developed high blood pressure – and it remained high for the rest of their lives. The rats' brain control over their nervous system and cardiovascular system was also permanently affected. So what can you do?

SERVE UP SOMETHING FISHY

Oily fish such as salmon, sardines, herring, mackerel and tuna are all rich in omega-3 fatty acids; canned tuna, though, is not a good source. Other excellent sources are walnuts, beans, olive oil and squashes. Fish oil is the most potent source of omega 3 as it is in a form that the body can readily use (both DHA and EPA).

SEEDS OF HOPE

Several seeds are also great sources of omega 3. Kiwi fruit seeds and flaxseed (sometimes called linseeds) are especially good sources. However, plant sources offer only ALA which the body has to convert before it can be used.

Children who take stimulant medication may lose their appetites. If you're having difficulty getting your child to eat dinner, let alone meet any oily fish targets, IDEA 33, *Food for thought*, may help.

Try another idea...

When people don't eat enough omega-3 fatty acids, they may be at greater risk of whatever kind of brain disorder they're innately or genetically or environmentally predisposed to. It can add fuel to the fire.
DR JOSEPH HIBBELIN, Psychiatrist and Lipid Biochemist, National Institutes of Health, Bethesda, Maryland

Defining idea...

83

How did it go?

Q **I'm a busy working mother of three, and my middle son has ADHD. My son doesn't like fish and I'm looking for a quick way to get his omega-3 levels up without using supplements. What do you suggest?**

A *There are two quick solutions. First, use a coffee grinder to prepare a mixture of ground pumpkin seeds, sunflower seeds, sesame and flaxseeds. Sprinkle this mix on cereals, on top of sandwich fillings and on salads. Secondly, see if he will take a spoonful of flaxseed oil every day. It doesn't taste of much and you could also use it in salad dressing.*

Q **Are fish oil capsules a good alternative to natural sources?**

A *The jury's still out on this one. My own view is that natural is better wherever possible. One problem with omega-3 oils is that they are unable to withstand heat once extracted. This means that you can cook food and it retains its omega-3 levels, but once it is taken out of food and used in supplements, it's an unstable chemical compound. There has been some research in New Zealand which indicated that some fish oil supplements are of questionable quality and a few may even be harmful.*

Q **My son's specialist has prescribed methylphenidate. Can he take fish oil capsules instead?**

A *Dietary supplementation with fish oils improves ADHD-related symptoms in at least some children. However, much more research in this area is needed. Omega 3 is not supported by current best evidence as a key treatment for ADHD. Speak to your specialist about using fish oils concurrently, but they should not be considered as an alternative to medication.*

20

Drug holidays

Stimulant drugs like Ritalin don't have to be taken every day to be beneficial.

In fact, having a weekend or school holiday off medication could be a good idea.

Experts disagree about whether medication for ADHD should be taken on weekends and in the holidays as well as during the school year. I've found that this depends on the child. Many children benefit from medication on weekends, others don't find it necessary. It's important to keep in mind that these drugs are not a cure for ADHD, but that they do help children focus, attend to what people are saying, be less squirmy and fidgety and less likely to blurt things out. It's also worth remembering that most stimulant medications used for treating ADHD are short-term medications. This means they work only when the medication is in your child's bloodstream and acting on the brain.

Depending on the type of medication, this period can be anywhere from four to twelve hours. Once this time has elapsed, stimulant medication is no longer effective. Stimulant medication is different to other drugs like antibiotics, antidepressants or the contraceptive pill, where a consistent period of medication is needed to be effective.

Here's an idea for you... **The school holidays can be a good time to evaluate how much of a difference medication is making. Taking a drug holiday during a school holiday, and monitoring concentration, attention and impulsive behaviour during this break, will give you a good idea of how your child is managing.**

So while it might seem counterintuitive not to be taking medication for a long-standing condition every day, you'll understand that it also makes sense to take it when it's most needed. For many children, the time their ADHD causes most problems is in school. At the weekends they can kick back a bit, and don't need to focus quite so hard, so it makes sense to take a break from medication then.

It can be a good idea for children to have a break from stimulants if they are causing side effects, such as trouble gaining weight – some time off of medication may give your child a chance to catch up with weight gain. An occasional drug holiday can also be helpful when determining if your child even needs to continue taking medication.

There are four main advantages of a drug holiday:
- It gives a break from any side effects.
- There's an opportunity for catching up with growth if growth suppression has been an issue.
- Your child can regain a lost appetite.
- There's a chance to see what the child is like off medication and re-evaluate whether it is still useful.

Many experts feel drug holidays are unimportant. Their view is that ADHD medication is safe, and has been used for many years with no lasting difficulties, so there is no reason why children shouldn't take it all the time. This is a valid view, but it is also good for parents to know both sides of the story. Only you, your child and your specialist can work together to weigh up the pros and cons of a drug holiday for your child. Many parents prefer their child to take medication every day to help with inattention, poor concentration and overactivity, but others prefer that as little medication as possible is used. Quite a lot of children taking medication for ADHD are off it at weekends, during holidays or through the summer. This decision is normally made between parents and their specialist.

Some parents have found after a break like this that their child no longer needs the medication. Others are more convinced than ever that it is making a big difference. Remember that stimulant medication isn't in your child's system for very long, so you will be able to reap benefits as soon as it is restarted.

Drug holidays can be an ideal opportunity to ramp up non-drug ideas. Weekends and holidays are an ideal time to try out some suggestions in IDEA 4, *Move it*. If your child's appetite is returning, check out IDEA 19, *A fat lot of good*.

Try another idea...

If a child's appetite is affected by stimulant medication and he isn't putting on weight, a drug holiday is an ideal opportunity for him to catch up.
PROFESSOR JOHN SCOTT WERRY, ADHD expert

Defining idea...

How did
it go?

Q My grandson has ADHD and takes methylphenidate. My daughter gives this to him on school days, but not at the weekends or in the school holidays. This seems really odd to us. He often spends time at the weekend with me and his granddad, and is totally out of control and rude. We've seen him on medication and he's a different boy. How can we tell our daughter he needs the medication all the time?

A *It must be really frustrating to feel you are seeing your grandson at his worst and are unable to enjoy his company as much as you'd like to. It might help to remember that this type of medication is not a cure for ADHD, and it doesn't help with rudeness either. It will help your grandson focus and pay attention, and reduces impulsiveness and hyperactivity, which is most likely why he is taking it to help him perform well in school.*

Q I'm not sure if my daughter would be better off having drug holidays, drug-free time at the weekends or a daily dose. Can you help?

A *It's not a simple choice, but you're right to be thinking about this. I can't advise you without knowing more about your daughter, but the best person to help you make this decision is either a child and adolescent psychiatrist, consultant paediatrician or GP with a special interest in ADHD. Talk it through.*

21

The hyperactivity thermometer

It's easy to tell if children have a fever. Just pop a thermometer in the mouth. Measuring ADHD isn't so easy.

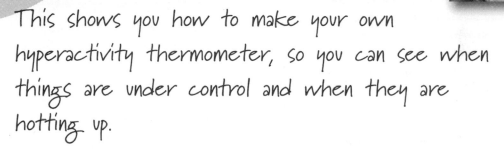

This shows you how to make your own hyperactivity thermometer, so you can see when things are under control and when they are hotting up.

It isn't fair really. We can measure children's height, weight, blood pressure and shoe size, but when it comes to measuring impulsivity, hyperactivity and concentration, there are no simple tools. But wouldn't it be great if there was a way of measuring hyperactivity, almost like a ruler for measuring how ADHD symptoms are from day to day? Well, there are ways you can measure your child's ADHD symptoms, and measure progress after ideas are put in place at school or at home.

The simplest way to do this is to make a hyperactivity thermometer. Draw a thermometer on a piece of cardboard and mark off regular intervals, numbering them from zero to ten. Laminate it, and make a few if you can. Calibrate your

Here's an idea for you...

Ask your child to rate their current position on the scale. As well as being more aware of good and bad days, the ADHD thermometer helps your child make changes. Ask questions like, 'what's stopping you from slipping one point lower down the scale?' to enable your child to identify strengths, and 'on a day when you are one point higher on the scale, what would tell you that it was a "one point higher" day?' and, to describe his ideal future, 'where on the scale would be good enough? What would a day at that point on the scale look like?'

child's hyperactivity thermometer like this. The scale on the thermometer ranges from the worst ADHD has ever been (zero) to the best things could ever possibly be (ten). Although real thermometers go up to a hundred, this measure tends to work well with school-age children who are used to having their schoolwork marked out of ten.

Before starting any new idea or intervention for ADHD, take a baseline level using the home hyperactivity thermometer. Describe ten to your child as 'feeling good, not being overactive, not getting into trouble for butting in, not being fidgety, being able to focus on work and get stuff done'. Zero is described as 'the most squirmy you can be, so bad you feel like running off, your mind is wandering all over the place and it's hard to remember what is going on'. Then ask: 'How many out of ten do you feel now?' Most children of six and over can use this sort of scale. Older children can dispense with the thermometer idea but can still rate attention, concentration and impulsivity out of ten. This baseline figure can then be used to monitor rises and falls in symptoms during school, homework time, leisure time and when trying a new medication or idea.

You can use these thermometers to measure the heat of various scenarios, not just ADHD symptoms. For instance, if your child is struggling to sit still at mealtimes, you could ask her something along these lines: 'On a scale of zero to ten, with zero being unable to sit still at all and having to fidget all the time and ten being completely successful at sitting still, how would you rate how you're doing with your problem right now? And when you rate yourself higher what will you be doing differently?'

Children who struggle with the concept of the thermometer may need extra support with maths. Check out IDEA 45, Summing it up.

Try another idea…

Clearly questions like this are a tool to measure progress. However, if young people have the ability to describe something as a problem, they also have the capacity to describe what better means. If they can describe this, they are able to describe that they also have what it takes to make it happen. Often children may see signs of a problem developing before it becomes an actual problem. By bringing small successes to their awareness, and helping them repeat the successful things they do when the problem is not there or is less severe, kids with ADHD become more confident about themselves and life becomes better. Plotting hyperactivity thermometer readings on a graph gives children a visual reminder of their progress over time.

We talked about whether we were going to be a thermometer or a thermostat. Are we just going to sit around and adjust to what's happening, or are we going to make it happen?
NICK GREENWELL, US sports coach

Defining idea…

91

How did
it go?

Q **My son has a learning disability as well as ADHD and numbers on a scale don't mean much to him. How can he use a scale like this?**

A *Children with learning disabilities may have difficulty with the concepts of conservation of number necessary for accurate use of a numerically based hyperactivity thermometer. You can use a hands thermometer instead. Zero is defined as hands together in front of you. The upper limit is described as arms as wide apart as you can get them. Physically demonstrate these limits and get your son to copy you if necessary. Then ask for his current level of feeling.*

Q **My daughter finds it difficult to rate her symptoms because she doesn't think there is anything wrong with her. I think she finds some things useful, because she tells me that people have started being nicer to her. What do you suggest?**

A *Many children with ADHD don't recognise that there is anything wrong with them. Why don't you have a scale of how nice people have been to your daughter, with ten being as friendly as possible and zero being completely unfriendly? This will give you a proxy measure of how her symptoms are impacting on her friendships.*

22

I like that

If your child does something well, and you recognise and reinforce that behaviour using a few kind words, he or she is likely to do it again.

Giving judicious praise is straightforward and it's hot. So hot it sizzles.

The most effective thing you can do to improve your child's behaviour is positive reinforcement. Scientific research has shown that children with ADHD hear more critical comments, gripes, negativity and put downs and less praise than their less active buddies and siblings. Now, this might not be the sort of research verdict that makes you fall off the toilet when you read it, but some great techniques developed from that research and while they are extremely potent, you don't have to be a brain scientist to use them.

Children with ADHD get less praise than children without ADHD. Hearing constant criticism erodes their self-esteem and they lose confidence in their ability to control their behaviour. When they do get praised, they are less likely to notice, and less likely to act on it.

Here's an idea for you...

Try the variable interval schedule with your child. Over the next couple of weeks, sometimes praise at the start of homework time, at other times praise when they're halfway through homework and the remaining times praise when they've finished homework. Before long you'll notice them sticking to their homework schedule better.

PRAISE OVERTIME

This means parents, carers and teachers of children with ADHD need to do 'praise overtime'. Find all the great behaviours you can and practise saying 'I like that' whenever you catch your child doing one of them. The real challenge is catching your child attending well to a task or person, not acting impulsively, persevering with something or doing something that requires a lot of concentration.

Just to get you started, these are a few of the things you might do 'praise overtime' for:

- Doing a jigsaw
- Playing quietly
- Sitting still
- Reading
- Colouring in
- Waiting his turn
- Being calm when provoked or upset

GET SPECIFIC

As well as noticing the desired behaviour, praise overtime means reinforcing these behaviours by letting your child know exactly what you liked and why. You might say something like: 'That was fantastic. I was so impressed when you sat quietly and read the rest of that chapter,' or 'I liked that. It would have been easy to give up with that difficult jigsaw but you kept going. That's really good' or 'Thank you for being so patient and waiting your turn at lunchtime today.'

DOING IT FOR THEMSELVES

Once you have mastered praise overtime, you can teach children how to reinforce good behaviours themselves. Try teaching your son or daughter to say 'I did that well' or 'I'm pleased with myself because…'. Rather than raising cocky kids, this helps rebuild self-esteem. Confident children who believe in themselves also believe in their ability to control their behaviour.

In order to understand how kids learn, psychologists experimented with rats. They set up a cage and a pellet dispenser, so rats were given pellets when they pressed a lever in the cage. Rats who were given a pellet every time they pressed the lever stopped pressing it when researchers stopped giving them pellets.

Try another idea…

Confident children are more able to inhibit their impulsive urges. Find out how to boost confidence in IDEA 35, *Everyone's a winner.*

Defining idea…

Words of praise, indeed, are almost as necessary to warm a child into a genial life as acts of kindness and affection. Judicious praise is to children what the sun is to flowers.
CHRISTIAN NESTELL BOVEE, American author and lawyer

Every ear is tickled with the sweet music of applause.
ISAAC BARROW, English clergyman, mathematician and classical scholar

Psychologists decided to find out what effect giving pellets at different intervals would have on rats learning to press a lever. They gave some rats pellets intermittently, other rats were given a pellet every five times they pressed the lever, a third group of rats were given a pellet every five minutes, regardless of whether they pressed the lever or not.

The most effective pellet-giving schedule was what they called *variable ratio*. This meant rats were given a pellet after pressing the lever, but they needed to press it a different number of times: sometimes five presses would work, sometimes seven, sometimes twenty-five. If it sounds too off the wall, just think of gambling. Adults buying lottery tickets or playing fruit machines are subject to variable ratio reinforcement. Most of the time you don't win, but the possibility of a jackpot keeps you going. And the small wins along the way, at unexpected times help reinforce the idea. Just like rats, children demonstrate consistently good behaviour when their behaviour is rewarded with praise or treats unexpectedly.

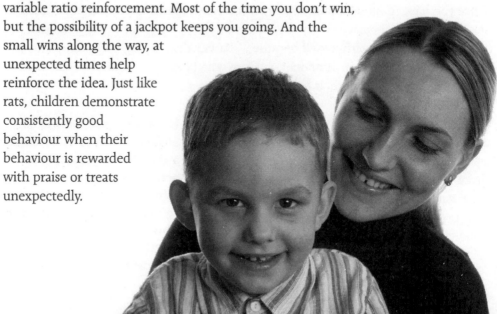

Q I find it really hard to give my son compliments. It sounds phoney to gush 'well done' all the time. Is it really necessary?

A *You're right that gushing with praise no matter what your child does is a bad idea. Indiscriminate praise won't help him distinguish good and bad behaviour. If and when he behaves well, noticing and praising will reinforce what he's doing. If you still feel awkward giving compliments, try giving him a hug, smile or nod, and let him know you are pleased.*

Q How long should we go on praising for? We started praising our son for sitting at the dinner table until everyone had finished eating. He seems to do this every evening now. Do we still need to praise him every night?

A *When your child is perfecting a new behaviour, it is best to reinforce this with praise every time he does it. New behaviours need immediate and continuous reinforcement to get embedded. But you're right, you don't need to keep praising him until he goes to university for sitting nicely at the table. Once he's got the hang of something, crank down the praise in that area and select another behaviour you want to reinforce.*

How did it go?

23

Forgiven, not forgotten

To be an effective caregiver of a child with ADHD you need to learn to practise forgiveness. It's incredibly hard, but has awesome power.

Forgiving your child and those around him can be one of the most powerful things you do. It's also one of the toughest ideas to implement.

World-renowned ADHD expert Russell Barkley is an advocate of practising forgiveness. He recommends that every day, after your ADHD child has gone to bed, parents ought to take five minutes to think back over the day and focus on all the times they felt angry, wronged or riled. Acknowledge any resentment, anger, disappointment, frustration and other painful emotions that have arisen. Let go of any destructive emotions that have come up during the day because of your child's behaviour or interruptions. Forgive your child, acknowledging that he is not always able to control his impulses or actions because of his ADHD.

Here's an idea for you...

Don't sweat the small stuff. A hypercontrolling attitude raises tension within families. It makes kids (and adults) want to rebel. If you turn into a hectoring control freak, fussing over every minor transgression, your child will be more likely to turn into a mini tyrant, and won't develop the independence necessary to function outside the family.

Be aware of difficult feelings and do all you can to let them go. When you breathe in, imagine you are taking in all the negative feelings and when you breathe out, imagine a wave of forgiveness enveloping your child. This is not the same as letting children off for bad behaviour, but without practising forgiveness, resentments will build up and it is harder to positively reinforce good behaviour.

Many parents misunderstand this last point and think that this is making excuses for their child, or letting them off the hook. Nothing could be further from the truth. This doesn't mean children with ADHD are not accountable for bad behaviour, nor that they can't be taught to make amends when they have done something wrong. This is separate from the act of adults forgiving them, which allows parents to move on and not be ground down by an ever-increasing list of misdemeanours.

After you have taken time to forgive your child, it's worth spending a moment forgiving those who have hurt or annoyed you by misunderstanding your child's behaviour: the woman in the supermarket checkout queue who told you 'he just needs a smack', the well-meaning friend who told you that you're just medicalising naughty behaviour. Remind yourself that these people are uneducated about ADHD and acting out of ignorance, not malice. Forgive those who have blamed you or criticised your parenting. It doesn't mean they are in the right, or getting away with it. There is a time and place for helping them understand about ADHD, but forgiving helps you move on past the hurt and anger and be the most effective parent you can be.

Teachers can also benefit from this. Find out more about working with schools to maximise your child's academic and social potential in IDEA 44, School's out.

Try another idea...

Before you go to bed, there's one more person to consciously forgive. Yourself. We all make mistakes every day. Nobody is a perfect parent and children with ADHD are often hard work to parent. Let's face it, they often bring out the worst in adults. Chances are that on most days you'll have made a couple of errors in managing your child, but there's no need to beat yourself up over this. Forgive yourself and let go of any guilt before your head hits the pillow. This doesn't mean that you don't need to keep aiming high and learning new tricks and techniques to help your child, but it does mean that you don't need to feel guilty, angry, resentful or ashamed about your actions. Forgiving doesn't mean you are giving yourself freedom to make the same mistakes, but it does mean going easier on yourself over the inevitable stuff ups. Replacing guilt with a resolve to put things right will make your parenting even more effective.

People don't change their behaviour unless it makes a difference for them to do so.
FRAN TARKENTON, American football player, businessman and author

Defining idea...

How did it go?

Q **It's all very well saying I ought to let go of negative emotions, but sometimes I feel I'm literally drowning in frustrations. What do you mean by letting go, and how can I achieve that?**

A *Good question. Try taking a deep breath in, and slowly exhale. This time imagine the anger and frustration leaving your body as you breathe out. Some people find it helpful to do something more vigorous, like going for a hard, fast run; others find soothing music helps to calm them. Experiment until you find how to banish those frustrations.*

Q **Try as I might, I just can't forgive my son's father. I feel cross with him every day. I'm convinced he has ADHD himself and has transmitted this to our son through his genes. He looks after my son at weekends and just does everything wrong. It takes until midweek to get my boy back on course and I'm seething with anger most of the time. How can I move forward?**

A *Forgiving your son's dad doesn't mean that you are permitting him to continue what sounds like poor parenting or at least undermining your efforts. He may be acting out of ignorance, and inviting him to the next follow-up appointment with your son's specialist may be a good start. ADHD does have a hereditary component, and if you are right and his father does also have it, maybe you could hold that in mind when you forgive him. If you feel very stuck and angry, consider talking to a professional. It is really hard and sometimes an outside view can turn things around. Good luck.*

24

Getting homework done

Many teenagers with ADHD have difficulty with homework because of shorter attention spans, restlessness and poor concentration.

Discover how to develop a homework strategy that still leaves time to relax and do fun things.

Pass these ideas on to your teenager:

By the book. Use a homework book. Minds are great for having ideas, but less good for storing information. There's no need to rely on your mind to remember what homework you have, and when it is due in. A homework book is much better for that.

Before leaving school. Set a reminder on your mobile phone to go off before you leave school. Use this prompt to make sure you have everything you need to complete your homework packed in your bag. If there was something you weren't sure about, now's the time to check. And clean out your locker every Friday. Get into the habit of bringing home all the loose papers in your locker that day. When you get home you can sort through them to see what you need, and having a clean locker will help you to stay organised and prepared.

Here's an idea for you...

Use your homework book to keep lists of things to do. Don't make lists on scraps of paper or you may end up losing or forgetting them. Get into the habit of completing a list of things to do each evening for what you want to accomplish the next day.

Clear the decks. Set up an area in your room that is just for homework. It's hard to get anything done if you spend lots of time trying to find things on your desk. Clear the homework space at the end of every session and keep pens, pencils, calculators and other stationery bits and pieces in a drawer. Now you won't end up using homework time to get organised.

Wired for success. Get a wire in-tray. At the end of every day, empty your school bag, pockets, inside pocket, back pocket, sports bag and pencil case of every loose bit of paper into the wire basket. Take out the papers one at a time and ask yourself what you need to do with it. Chances are you will either need to file it, bin it or act on it. If you need to act on it, you have to decide if you need to do something there and then, or if you need to do it later. If you have something you need to do but you don't need to do immediately, put the date you plan to do it in your homework book.

Daylight saving. Aim to get all your homework done while it is still light if possible. There's good evidence suggesting that the same homework takes longer in the small hours.

Hit the hard stuff. Do your hardest homework or your least favourite subject first. Once it's out of the way, you'll feel better. Saving dreaded homework for later often means you're more likely to dawdle with your other homework and put it off. Plan to take a five-minute break every half hour and then get back to work.

Cue cards. Use index cards to record key facts when you are revising for exams. Making these little cards will help you break information down into small chunks, which are easier to take in and remember. The great thing about them is that they are portable. Take them around with you and have a look at them whenever you are waiting for someone.

Chunk it up. If you have big projects or coursework, it can feel very daunting and many people are tempted to put those off. The best thing for those bigger projects is to break them down into small chunks and make a timetable for completing each item. Keep your timetable on the wall of your homework area so you can see it every day and tick the chunks off.

Great mates. Befriend some boffins and keep a list of their numbers in your homework area. If you get stuck or your attention keeps wandering, call or text someone who might be able to help you.

Reward yourself. Agree some privileges with your parents as a reward for sticking to the homework strategy. Examples of privileges might be renting a DVD at the weekend, having extra time on the internet, inviting a friend for a sleepover or credit for your phone.

It can be hard finding time to do homework and fun things in the evenings and weekends. **IDEA 27, *Every second counts*, can help you manage time.**

Try another idea...

Children have to be educated, but they have also to be left to educate themselves.
ERNEST DIMNET, *The Art of Thinking*

Defining idea...

How did it go?

Q   **I've been working hard to get this stuff in place, but my mum still insists on checking my homework every night. She picks around at it and is really bossy about me changing things. Surely the teachers want to see my homework, not hers. How do I get her to back off?**

A   *It's probably the last thing you want to hear, but she has your interests at heart and wants you to do well. Some mums find it hard to butt out of homework, especially when they've been involved in it for years. You might have to do some compromising. Put a deal to her. If your marks improve consistently over the next month, she agrees to leave you to do your homework unaided. I think you made a good point about teachers wanting to see your work. When you're feeling calm, tell her you appreciate her help, but that you want your work marked, not hers. Try to keep her in the loop by asking for her help with revision for tests.*

Q   **I'm really easy to distract when I'm doing my homework. Is there anything you can suggest?**

A   *Start your homework by turning off email, instant messaging and your phone, and that will help protect you against being distracted. Only switch your phone on if you need to contact your helpful boffin, and switch it off again once you have finished talking about your work.*

25

It's all about me

Kids with ADHD have extraordinary pressures: school can seem twice as tough, it's harder to make and keep friends and they often feel everyone is at them for bad behaviour.

Whether your child has had a tough day, or is overcome with frustrations over homework or friends, these seriously soothing suggestions will help the most wound-up kid chill out.

There are a number of cool techniques your child can use to relax when the pressures of ADHD feel overwhelming.

GETTING YOUR BREATH BACK

When stress levels rise, breathing speeds up and becomes shallower. By becoming aware of their breathing and learning to slow it down, children with ADHD can become more in control and feel relaxed.

There are two ways of learning how to do this. Ask your child to put his left hand on his tummy, just over his belly button. Next get him to cover his left hand with his right hand. Get him to breathe in slowly and notice his tummy rising under his

Here's an idea for you... **If your child is having difficulty winding down or relaxing, find a quiet place where he won't be disturbed, and get him to close his eyes. Ask him to cast his mind back to the time he felt most deeply relaxed. Ask him to imagine himself in that calming place now. Encourage him to bring it to life vividly, using all his senses. What can he see, hear, taste, smell and feel? Now encourage him to stay there for as long as it takes to feel calm. One of the great things about children with ADHD is that they are often good at visualising and imagining their calming place, so they have an individualised portable stress-buster.**

hands, pushing them up. When he breathes out, he will notice his hands falling. See if you can encourage him to do this, breathing in and out slowly and noticing his hands rise and fall, about a dozen times. The aim is to get him to focus on his breathing and be more aware of it, not to change it. Once he has done this exercise a few times, he will be able to use it when he is tense, and it will help the muscles in his face and around his jaw relax. As he breathes more deeply, his arms and legs will feel less tense too.

SHOWING SOME MUSCLE

Progressive Muscle Relaxation relaxes the body progressively as children focus on different muscle groups. There are three basic steps:
- Isolate a muscle, inhale and tense it.
- Hold the muscle tense for five to ten seconds.
- Exhale, and slowly relax the tense muscle. This relaxation phase needs to be at least as long as the tensing phase, possibly longer.

The progressive tense–hold–relax sequence moves up or down through the body. Some children prefer to move from toes and feet up towards their face. Others prefer to move down from the head, beginning with scrunching their eyes up and working down the body. Here's how to put it into practice:

- Ask your child to lie down.
- Get him to bend his legs at the knees so both feet are flat on the ground.
- Say, 'close your eyes and pretend you are at the beach, lying on the sand.'
- Ask him to pretend he can hear the water lapping against the shore.
- Ask him to imagine that it's a beautiful, sunny day. The sun feels warm against his skin and the sand is warm underneath him.
- Have your child take a few deep breaths as he 'watches the waves go in and out'.
- Now ask him to squeeze the sand between his toes. Inhale, hold, exhale, relax.
- Now squeeze both feet. Inhale, hold, exhale, relax.
- Say, 'Do you feel the difference when you are relaxed?'
- Now get him to tighten his legs. Inhale, hold, exhale, relax.
- Now his bottom, tummy, and chest. Inhale, hold, exhale, relax.
- Now his hands and arms.
- Then his shoulders and neck. Inhale, hold, exhale, relax.
- And then the face. Sometimes children don't know how to tense up the face. You may need to say something like 'screw your eyes shut'. Inhale, hold, exhale, relax.
- Finally, have him squeeze his whole body. Inhale, hold, exhale, relax.
- Ask him to take a few more deep breaths.
- Remind him to feel the warm sun and sand, and hear the water lap against the shore.
- And ask your child to open his eyes.

Drawing can help children with ADHD chill out and relax. Check out some other benefits in IDEA 49, *Drawing together*.

Try another idea...

There is no need to go to India or anywhere else to find peace. You will find that deep place of silence right in your room, your garden or even your bathtub.
DR ELISABETH KUBLER-ROSS, psychiatrist and author

Defining idea...

How did it go?

Q **My daughter really lost it in the supermarket the other day, and ended up crying with frustration. I tried to calm her down and teach some deep breathing, but it just didn't work. I don't think she can relax. What can I do?**

A *The time for learning relaxation exercises is, paradoxically, when children are relatively calm and relaxed. Trying to teach her new techniques when she's already stressed could make things worse. If she learns and practises relaxation techniques when she is calm, she will become confident with them and able to call on her repertoire of relaxation when she is under fire.*

Q **My teenage son could really do with chilling out, but I don't think reading him a beach scene is going to cut it. Any suggestions?**

A *There are lots of things you could do. You could give him this, explain it might be a bit too babyish for him, but that the principles could be worth a shot. Alternatively you could make him a tape of the beach scene that he can listen to before going to bed. Use words like abdomen instead of tummy and he probably won't find it condescending.*

26

Assertive parenting

Choose a parenting style that reflects a commitment to your child's independence without compromising on rules and fair play.

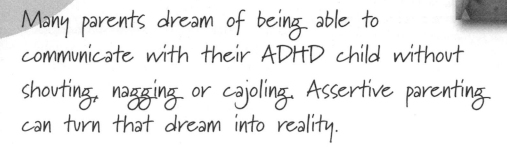

Many parents dream of being able to communicate with their ADHD child without shouting, nagging or cajoling. Assertive parenting can turn that dream into reality.

Researchers have outlined three different parenting styles:
- Permissive
- Aggressive
- Assertive

You're unlikely to fall into one of these categories all the time, but most parents veer towards one of them. Here are some illustrations to help.

Here's an idea for you...

Say no. If your child is doing something and you don't want him to do it, a short, brisk 'no' can be very effective. Be as brief and brisk as you can, avoiding flimflam, tearful pleas or an explanation of why you are saying no. Cultivate a neutral tone of voice. This type of reprimand is highly effective.

PERMISSIVE PARENTING

Permissive parents often find it hard to enforce rules and their kids frequently get the upper hand. They are sometimes scared to be more authoritative in case they lose their child's love or friendliness, or annoy their partner.

John is a single dad who has his son Warwick on alternate weeks. Warwick has ADHD. John is fairly laid back, and wants Warwick to enjoy some of the things he didn't have. When Warwick is boisterous and challenging, John is sometimes a bit intimidated by him. Their Sunday evening can go a bit like this:

John: Warwick, it's time to go to your mother's. Haven't you packed up your stuff yet?
Warwick: No, Dad, I'm playing PlayStation. We can go when I've finished this game.
John: But don't you remember we were late last time and I promised your mother we'd get you back on time this weekend?
Warwick: You're spoiling my game, Dad. Just let me finish this.
John: Whatever, Warwick. Just let me know when you're ready and I'll drive you back.

AGGRESSIVE PARENTING

Putting your needs above your child's all the time isn't a sustainable solution. Parents who are exceptionally strict about rules and use threats and harsh punishments are setting themselves up for a rebellious backlash.

Single dad Alvin has his ADHD son Dwayne on alternate weeks. This is their Sunday evening:

Alvin: Dwayne, it's time to go. Haven't you packed up your stuff yet?
Dwayne: No, I'm playing PlayStation.
Alvin: You're such a lazy good for nothing. If I'd spoken to my father like that, he'd have thrashed me to within an inch of my life.
Dwayne: Dad, you're so mean. Can't I just finish this game?
Alvin: Go to your room now and pack. And I mean now.

ASSERTIVE PARENTING

There's a lot to be said for standing up for your ideas and desires and doing this in an understandable, short, sensible and sensitive way. Assertive parenting means your child is less likely to be dependent on you and will be better able to think for himself and control impulsive behaviour.

Assertive parenting also means acting in a consistent manner. Find out how in IDEA 12, Home uniform.

Try another idea...

Never allow a person to tell you no who doesn't have the power to say yes.
ELEANOR ROOSEVELT

Defining idea...

Frank is another single dad. His son Neville also stays alternate weeks. Frank wants Neville to think for himself, and not be limited by his ADHD. Here's their Sunday evening:

Frank: Neville, it's time to go. Have you packed up?
Neville: No, Dad, I'm playing PlayStation. I'll pack when I've finished this game.
Frank: Neville, we did a deal before dinner. You were going to play while I cooked and then pack after dinner, instead of getting ready at the usual time.
Neville: But I'm nearly at Level 8. Can't I have just two more tries?
Frank: I know it's annoying when you're so close, but we did a deal and I also did a deal with your mum to have you back in time.

Being an assertive parent takes a bit of practice. Here are ten tips:
1. Say what you mean.
2. Mean what you say.
3. Make eye contact before reminding a child of a deal or the rules.
4. Instead of asking your child to do something, remind him of an agreement.
5. If a child tries to talk you out of something, stick to your agreement.
6. Express your needs clearly and directly.
7. Express your ideas without feeling browbeaten or guilty.
8. Cultivate self-reliance and independence.
9. Persist until you get all the services your child needs.
10. Develop a positive attitude.

Q   **I try my best to do these assertive communication styles, but my daughter spends a lot of time with her dad. My ex lets her do what she wants. He finds it hard to be assertive, and I don't think it is good for her to have these different styles. What do you suggest?**

How did it go?

A   *Parents are different and often do things differently, even if they are together. One ruse you might try is using some of your assertive parenting techniques on your ex-partner. Catch him 'doing things right', and catch him 'not doing things wrong'. Offer praise. For example: 'I noticed that you didn't allow her to get away with not doing any homework this weekend. I appreciate you working with me on this.'*

Q   **I get very angry sometimes, and end up shouting at my son when he is into everything and hyper. I really want to be assertive, but end up getting mad instead. Can you help?**

A   *The four As of anger management might. The first is **A**wareness – anger is a natural human feeling. Everyone feels it, we just don't all express it appropriately. Then comes **A**cceptance – you are responsible for your own feelings. If you expect someone else to be responsible for your happiness, you will always be disappointed. Then **A**nalysis – you get angry at what happened, so separate the situation from the person. Your son didn't 'make' you angry. Finally, **A**ppropriate action – deal with issues assertively when they arise, when you feel the feelings. It's normal to get angry, but the trick is to develop a positive, assertive style of expressing it.*

27
Every second counts

Wouldn't it be fantastic to swap the feeling of being overwhelmed for calm control? Imagine parenting your child effectively, seemingly in direct proportion to your ability to relax.

If you learn to make every second count together, you'll be a more effective parent and your child will be planning school and home projects with ease.

Many parents with a hyperactive child become so busy they don't know where their time goes. Keeping an activity diary is one way of establishing a baseline of what you do. Spend a week finding out where your time really goes by recording what you are doing every ten minutes. If you are interrupted during a task, write down what the interruption was and who interrupted you. Doing this exercise requires a great deal of effort and commitment, but is a fantastic investment. At the end of the week, review your diary and look for any patterns of activity. What causes delays? Who interrupts you most? What's missing? Do you have time for fun, lunch breaks, coffee with friends, exercise and relaxation?

Here's an idea for you... **David Allen claims his 'two-minute rule' adds six months to your life. If the next action takes less than two minutes, do it straight away. When you're overwhelmed, blitz through several 'two-minute actions', rapidly regaining control. This approach appeals to minds that stray easily and fly from topic to topic.**

Making minor changes to the things that waste most of your time can make a big difference. Think about what is really important to you, both to yourself as a parent and for you as a family, and see how you can restructure your day to make time for those things. For example, if your evenings are spent being interrupted by your child rather than relaxing and you wish you had time to exercise together, you might consider enrolling her in an exercise class. Plan to exercise together once a week, instead of trying to fit it into already busy (but unproductive) evenings.

GETTING THERE

David Allen has spent twenty-five years helping people achieve stress-free efficiency. He has been called one of the world's most influential thinkers on productivity, yet refers to himself as 'the laziest person you've ever met'. So lazy, he insists, that he developed a way of getting things done with 'less effort, more ease and elegance'.

The systematic approach he devised can easily be adapted to a household or classroom and I believe it's ideally suited to those with ADHD. In essence, he suggests keeping an inventory of all commitments, organised and reviewed in a systematic way so you can focus and trust your gut instincts about what to do at any moment. There are a couple of basic principles.

Capturing anything that has your attention. David Allen advocates carrying a 'note-capturing device' for corralling ideas. This is a perfect solution for kids with ADHD who are likely to have lots of impulses that they need a way of managing and tracking, allowing them to decide later whether they will act on them. Once you or your child have written a new idea down, put it in an in-tray which gets processed at least once a day.

Defining the next step. Once you've captured thoughts, identify the next step to move towards your desired outcome. These are 'next actions'. Allen recommends grouping them by context. Instead of traditional 'to do' lists, his adherents have lists called 'at home', 'at office', 'calls' and even 'at spouse'. Your child's contexts will probably be something like: 'at school', 'at home' and 'at computer'. She can get into the habit of looking at these prompt sheets when she is in the relevant place.

Regular long weekends away are an essential part of being able to thrive as a parent of an ADHD child. Find out why in IDEA 29, *Recharge your batteries.*

Try another idea...

One guy's five-year-old son couldn't tidy his room. They gathered everything in the room and put it in a big box. Then they took things out one by one, deciding where it went or what to do with it. The kid loved the game. The box was critical. It allowed the boy to corral stuff so his brain could focus on one thing at a time.
DAVID ALLEN, productivity guru

Defining idea...

How did it go?

Q **If I am to get to work for 9 a.m., I have to be out of the house by 8.15 so I can drop my son off at school first. Despite my best efforts, he dawdles in the mornings and I get stressed as we are always running late. How can I get him to be a little faster?**

A *Save time in the morning by changing the way you organise his bedroom. Instead of having a drawer for underwear, a drawer for socks, a drawer for jumpers and so on, have dedicated drawers for school wear, after-school wear, sports, weekends and so on. This way he only has to go to one drawer.*

Q **I'm a single mum who works full time. My son has ADHD and has never slept particularly well, naturally waking at about 5.30 a.m. My sleep has never been that great either but I make up for it by having a lie-in at the weekends. Or I used to. Now my son wakes me in the small hours demanding breakfast and playtime. How can I get some extra sleep?**

A *A proven ruse that gets you an occasional lie-in is constructing snail trails between your child's bedroom and yours. Your son follows the trail, which is punctuated by toys, games, puzzles, word searches, books, snacks and drinks. If you get it right, it could take him a stimulating hour to make this short journey. Prizes for correct puzzles help, especially if you throw in a couple of tricky questions.*

28

Eliminate additives

Bouncing off the wall after fizzy drinks or brightly coloured sweets? Eliminating additives from your child's diet could drive down levels of hyperactivity.

Scientists have recently shown what many parents long suspected. Food additives seem to worsen hyperactive behaviour.

Several food additives could worsen hyperactivity in children, concluded a scientific paper in the journal *The Lancet*. In the study, Jim Stevenson, a professor of psychology at the University of Southampton, and his colleagues gave drinks containing additives to 297 children. The children were in two groups: three-year-olds, and eight- and nine-year-olds. The drinks contained artificial food colouring and additives such as sodium benzoate, a preservative, and were similar to commercially available ones. The amount of additives was also similar to what is found in one or two servings of confectionery a day, according to the report. As a comparison, some children were given drinks without additives. Over the six weeks of the trial, Stevenson's team found that children in both age groups who drank the drinks containing additives displayed significantly more hyperactive behaviour. These children also had shorter attention spans.

For the next month, check all labels rigorously and cut out foods containing the following E numbers from your child's diet: E102, E104, E110, E122, E124, E129, E211 (you may find them listed by name instead). At the end of the month, review any difference in behaviour. It might be worth having a permanent ban on them.

However, which specific additives caused specific behavioural problems is not known. Other additives assessed in the study included a number of colourings – sunset yellow (E110); carmoisine (E122), a red colouring; ponceau 4R (E124), another red; tartrazine (E102); quinoline yellow (E104) and allura red AC (E129), an orange-red food dye.

One of the additives, sodium benzoate, has been linked to cell damage in other studies, and to an increased risk of cancer. Sodium benzoate is found in most colas, many fruit drinks as well as in some salad dressings and table sauces. It's also called E211; try to avoid it.

Let's look at some of the other E numbers to avoid in more detail:

- **E102 or tartrazine:** found in soft drinks, ice cream, sweets, fish fingers, cakes and biscuits. This is a synthetic dye which has been linked to serious allergic reactions and to anxiety, migraine and blurred vision. It has been said to cause hyperactivity and is banned in Austria and Norway.
- **E104 or quinoline yellow:** used in sweets and soft drinks. Another synthetic dye, derived from coal tar, which has been linked to skin rashes and hyperactivity as well as temper tantrums. It's banned in the US, Australia, Norway and Japan.

■ **E110 or sunset yellow:** used in sweets, yoghurts and cheap jams. This is a coal tar dye. It has been blamed for causing upset stomachs, skin swelling and hyperactivity. Norway, Finland and Sweden have banned it.

■ **E122 or carmoisine:** this may be present in sweets, yoghurts, marzipan and cake mixes. It's another coal tar dye which has links with hyperactivity and has also been linked with nettle rash and water retention. Banned in Norway, Sweden, the US and Japan.

■ **E124 or ponceau 4R:** found in sweets, tinned fruit, jellies, desserts, cakes, some over-the-counter medicines like cough syrup and in vitamins. It's also derived from coal tar. It is said to cause hyperactivity and worsen asthma and has been banned by Norway and the US.

■ **E129 or allura red:** this is often present in sweets, soft drinks and condiments and is common in cosmetics. A coal tar-derived dye, it's been linked to hyperactivity. Norway and Australia have banned it.

If you're keen to find out how food could improve your child's symptoms, check out IDEA 19, *A fat lot of good.*

Try another idea...

We changed our son's diet and, when he went back to school after the holidays, teachers assumed he was on drug therapy.
NICK GIOVANELLI, parent and helper with the Hyperactive Children's Support Group, London

Defining idea...

123

Defining idea...

It's like Jekyll and Hyde when my son eats additives. I am housebound when he has eaten them.

HELEN BUNIAK, social worker and parent of a child with ADHD

Though some countries have banned some additives completely, they are not banned worldwide. Although the link between hyperactivity and additives in the *Lancet* paper is alarming, the scientific community recognises that this is just one study. Another study in 2002 did not show a conclusive link between additives and hyperactivity, and without evidence from a number of different trials there is unlikely to be a widespread ban. The *Lancet* paper has been criticised because children were given a drink with a mixture of additives and this is not how they would consume them in reality. It also did not show conclusively which particular additive was responsible for hyperactivity. For these reasons, it's unlikely there'll be a worldwide ban. So the onus is on parents to see if their child seems to be worse with additives and eliminate them if necessary.

Q   **We've got into the habit of checking lists of ingredients and are being vigilant about additives. However, my son likes pick and mix. How can we find out what is in loose sweets?**

How did it go?

A   *Despite your best efforts, you won't be able to be certain about every food your child eats. Don't be disheartened, you're already making a big commitment by eliminating additives at home and it sounds as if you are noticing good results. Why not set up a pick and mix at home, using sweets which you know are dyed with natural colours?*

Q   **I'm careful at home but my daughter went to a birthday party and came back bouncing off the walls. The hosts assured me all the food was 'natural' but I really suspect she'd eaten some additives and was made worse by them. How can I be sure?**

A   *Parties can be difficult. As a general rule, I would be suspicious of any brightly coloured food, cake icing, jellies and any drinks that look brighter than squeezed fruit would look. You might not be able to change much at other people's birthday parties, however.*

29

Recharge your batteries

Parenting a child with ADHD is exhausting. Everyone who looks after an ADHD child feels drained from time to time and needs regular breaks to be effective.

Regular long weekends away are an essential part of being able to thrive as a parent of an ADHD child. Whether you detox or retox, a break is just what the doctor ordered.

ADHD aside, all adults and children need time to themselves. Any adult who looks after a child with ADHD needs that time more than ever, but they are often the first to forgo it. When you are taking care of somebody with ADHD, which can be exhausting, you also need to think about caring for yourself.

If you want to enjoy rewarding time with your child, treating yourself to regular adult-only time is the way to go. A good guideline is to have an evening every week and a full weekend every twelve weeks for yourself. There's no shame in seeking refuge in regular time away from your child. If you can find a sanctuary away from the demands of high-octane parenting, you'll be better equipped to rise to each challenge – and be more fun to be around, as well.

Here's an idea for you...

Make a block booking with a babysitter so you have an evening to yourself once a week. Although you may feel indulgent for taking time for yourself, regular refuelling and recharging will mean you have the energy to meet the extra parenting needs of children with ADHD.

Make a list of must-see and must-do experiences that you could fit into an evening or weekend, and then work your way through your list. Having something to look forward to will take the edge off difficult times. Similarly, thinking back to memorable experiences will help you relax and retain a sense of perspective when the going gets tough. However, getting away from it all takes a little planning. Commit yourself to a particular date and circle it on the calendar, then tell your family and make an action plan for a smooth getaway.

To make sure you can really switch off when you are away, consider leaving your child with a skilled professional carer, rather than leaning on your friends and family. If you need to arrange respite care it's a good idea to organise that first as there may be difficulties in booking a suitable place or services for the days you want – especially at popular holiday times. Then you can sort out your own break.

You can get respite care in two different ways:
- Residential respite: your child goes away to be looked after by someone else for a while.
- Domiciliary care: Someone comes into your home and takes over care for a while (a few hours or overnight) so you can go out and have some time to yourself.

Speak to your specialist about respite care, as you may be eligible for some financial assistance towards it. It probably won't cover the costs of one of those luxury hotels where you don't feel the slightest regret if you never leave the grounds, but it might pay for someone to look after your little one so you can get to your hotel without too much drama. Whatever else you do, leave behind contingency plans, essential contact numbers and agree the circumstances in which you can be contacted. Make a plan to call your child at set times and stick to them. With all these things in place, you'll be better able to kick back.

No time for a break? If you're struggling to get everything done, check out IDEA 27, *Every second counts*, for some ways to max every moment. Learn some relaxation techniques in IDEA 25, *It's all about me*.

Try another idea...

In most sports there is provision for time out. These breaks give the coach and team a chance to strategise, catch their breaths and re-enter the game with renewed energy. In our daily lives, there are very few scheduled time outs. Even coffee breaks are usually filled with stimulation rather than refreshment. Somewhere along the line, relaxation got dropped.
CAROLYN WEBSTER-STRATTON, Director of the Parenting Clinic, University of Washington

Defining idea...

How did it go?

Q **I'm home all day with my six-year-old who has ADHD. It's fine when he's at school, as I get a break, but in the holidays I get exhausted. He hasn't got many friends because he's so naughty, so he doesn't get invited round to play much. I do try to get away with my partner, but am dreading the next long holiday. I feel bad going away then and leaving him, after all, he's my responsibility. What do you think?**

A *He is your responsibility, and you are also responsible for looking after yourself. I suggest you book an afternoon babysitter on occasion during the holidays and have some time to relax.*

Q **My daughter's had a really difficult year since being diagnosed with ADHD and anxiety. She's hard work at times, but I love her dearly. I also feel dreadfully selfish about going away with my partner, who isn't her dad. When I return, I do feel more relaxed, but the guilt almost eats me up when I'm away. Is it really worth it?**

A *There's no need to feel guilty or selfish for looking after your own needs. If you are refreshed, you'll be better able to meet your daughter's high level of needs. You're also showing your child that you know how to take care of yourself, which is an important lesson for her to observe. Regular breaks turn frazzled parents into serious hotshot ninjas. Simple as that.*

30

Double whammy

Children with ADHD are much more likely to have a host of other medical conditions. Around two-thirds of clinically referred kids with ADHD do.

Having a second diagnosis is called co-morbidity. Discovering a double whammy can feel like the end of the world, but is actually an important new window of opportunity.

Up to half of all children diagnosed with ADHD also have conduct disorder, and a quarter also have anxiety problems. About a fifth also have learning problems and as many as a third have delayed motor development. Astute parents and teachers need to be aware of which signs to be alert for, and know what to do if they spot them.

The common conditions that often co-exist with ADHD include:
- Oppositional defiant disorder.
- Conduct disorder.
- Learning disabilities.
- Anxiety and depression.

131

Here's an idea for you...

If you have any concerns that there may be more than ADHD going on, don't be afraid of asking for a second opinion to help you get an accurate diagnosis. Make a note of your child's behaviours, and write down what he thinks about and share this information with the specialist. You might like to ask his teacher to provide a short report of his academic and social performance, too.

OPPOSITIONAL DEFIANT DISORDER

As many as a third of children with ADHD have oppositional defiant disorder (ODD). These children are often defiant, stubborn, non-compliant, have outbursts of temper or become belligerent. They argue and refuse to obey. Family work and early behavioural interventions are often useful, and it is important to address oppositional defiant disorder early because it can lead to serious problems in future if left unchecked.

CONDUCT DISORDER

About 20–40% of ADHD children may develop conduct disorder. This is a serious pattern of antisocial behaviour. Children with conduct disorder frequently lie or steal, get into fights or pick on other children. Not surprisingly, they run a high risk of getting into trouble with the police. They are aggressive towards people and sometimes also to animals, destroy property, break into homes, steal, set fires and don't often appear on birthday party invitation lists. They are at increased risk for both experimenting with and becoming dependent on alcohol and other drugs.

LEARNING DISABILITIES

Many children with ADHD also have a learning disability. These disabilities include difficulty understanding certain sounds or words or difficulty in expressing themselves in words. In school-age children, reading or spelling disabilities, writing disorders and arithmetic disorders may appear. A type of reading disorder, dyslexia, is quite widespread. Children with both ADHD and a learning disability often need to concentrate especially hard in order to learn compensatory skills – and such intense concentration does not come easily to them. For this reason, many specialists are more inclined to use medication early on for children with both conditions, so they can be helped to concentrate and focus while learning vital skills.

Discovering you have more than one diagnosis to deal with can feel isolating and overwhelming, so share the load – see IDEA 31, *Get in a gang*. If your child is having difficulty making friends, check out IDEA 22, *I like that*, to encourage more sociable behaviour.

Try another idea...

Without deviation from the norm, progress is not possible.
FRANK ZAPPA

Defining idea...

ANXIETY AND DEPRESSION

Some children often have anxiety or depression as well. It is important to have this diagnosed as a child will be better able to cope with having ADHD if anxiety or depression is treated.

Teasing these diagnoses apart can be complex, as many have overlapping symptoms, and almost every condition that can coexist with ADHD can also mimic it. If any of the above sound as if they might apply to your child, finding a specialist who is experienced in assessing children with neuropsychiatric conditions is important. Accurate diagnosis is vital in shaping an appropriate treatment plan.

Finally, do remember that many children with ADHD have immature interpersonal skills, a tendency towards egocentric and selfish behaviour, poor awareness of and regard for consequences of their own behaviour, low frustration tolerance, increased sensitivity to environmental stimuli and exaggerated emotional reactions anyway. That doesn't mean they have any of the other problems, though children with ADHD are much more likely to have a host of other medical conditions. The common manifestations of ADHD don't do much for popularity in the playground, however.

Q   **My son seems very slow to pick things up and I am worried he may have a learning disability. How can we find out and what can be done?**

How did it go?

A   *Children with ADHD often learn more slowly than their contemporaries. To know for certain, he needs to have a special evaluation by a psychologist. This can be arranged through school or by your medical specialist. The psychologist needs to be trained in evaluating children with ADHD and learning disability. Find out first and take it from there.*

Q   **My grandson is in trouble with the police a lot. In the last month he has been caught for joyriding, fire setting and stealing. He was diagnosed with ADHD by a specialist, but surely this is just juvenile delinquency and medication won't help. What do you think?**

A   *You're quite right, his behaviour is delinquent, but that doesn't mean he hasn't got ADHD too. There is good evidence from scientific studies suggesting that he ought to be treated for his impulsive, hyperactive and inattentive tendencies. When these are under control, the delinquent behaviour is likely to decrease too. This isn't to say that ADHD is an excuse for what he is doing, nor that he has no control over it. Most children with ADHD will not get in trouble with the law.*

31

Get in a gang

Support groups can be a lifeline. Other parents can share strategies, information, advice and support, and they really know what you're going through.

Setting up a support group for other parents whose children have ADHD can seem like a daunting prospect. Here's how to set one up that provides real support.

The opportunity to meet and talk with other parents can help make the task of parenting a child with ADHD easier. Groups have other purposes too, and a support group for parents whose children have ADHD can offer many benefits...

- **Receiving and building up personal support.** Bringing up a child with ADHD can feel isolating or stigmatising. It can be difficult for many parents to discuss the disorder with family and friends, who may not understand. Meeting other parents can often help you to share experiences and feelings. You can gain considerably and will be relieved to find that others share the same challenges.
- **Gaining knowledge.** ADHD children are often misunderstood, misdiagnosed or labelled as naughty. The benefits of attending a support group include being able to learn strategies from invited experts and sharing possible ways of managing symptoms.

Here's an idea for you...

When you launch your support group, consider getting some local publicity. Contact the health correspondents of local papers and see if you can get them interested in doing a story about ADHD and mentioning your group.

■ **Giving support.** Attending a support group is a two-way process. Every parent there can make some contribution to the group which will benefit others, whether it be a personal experience or an new idea. Being a part of a group, either active or not, is important in itself.

Finally, seeing parents who have faced the same challenges with their child that you are facing with yours, and who have since progressed, is an invaluable gift of hope.

RUNNING A GROUP

Well-organised groups are few and far between, so if you want to revive one, or set one up from scratch, this ought to help.

Thought needs to be given to timetabling of groups so that they fit in with both school and family life. Once you've identified suitable times, you might want to approach local government or charities for a small grant to cover running costs. To do this you will need to set up a bank account and have a constitution. The aims of your group may be something like:

■ To raise awareness about ADHD.
■ To promote good relationships between parents, their children, health services, social services and education.
■ To support parents with information, listening and practical ideas.

- To improve the quality of family life by helping parents support children with ADHD.
- To develop parents' skills.

Your rules might be something like:
- Accepting differences.
- No pressure to speak.
- Listening.
- Confidentiality.

If you're finding it difficult to make the time to attend a support group, investing ten minutes to read IDEA 27, *Every second counts*, could be the answer.

Try another idea...

The venue needs to be accessible, even to those without cars. Parents ought to be able to expect a welcoming environment which also feels private. Wherever the venue is, it should be prepared carefully before the parents arrive. The room should be comfortably warm with chairs arranged appropriately. Refreshments (cake, chocolate and fruit are popular) should be provided. If childcare is offered, it should be near or adjoining the venue to ensure people feel relaxed about leaving their children.

Speak to local specialists about how to best publicise your group and ask them to tell families they know about it. Some departments may be able to provide meeting space or photocopy fliers and posters for you. Put up posters in local doctors' practices and schools, explaining what the group is about and inviting people to join and contribute. Bear in mind that the most successful recruitment takes place through face-to-face contact and by word of mouth.

We must all hang together, or assuredly, we shall all hang separately.
BENJAMIN FRANKLIN

Defining idea...

139

When you're running a meeting of your group:

- Start on time.
- Introduce yourself.
- Outline the aims and rules.
- Emphasise confidentiality.
- This may be a time to discuss some aspect of ADHD. Some examples may include different treatments, individual experiences, medication issues and so on.
- At this stage you could open up the floor to members and give other parents an opportunity to talk.
- A guest speaker may give some formal focus to the evening. If you do invite outside speakers, nominate someone to make sure all equipment (flip charts, videos, overhead projectors) is in place. Any handouts should be presented on good-quality paper. It is a good idea to give each parent a file to store handouts.
- Close the meeting on an upbeat note, leaving members wanting to come back.
- Informal time at the end of the meeting gives members a chance to get to know each other.
- Suggest that members swap email addresses to stay in virtual contact between meetings. You could even have an online discussion forum if you have someone with these skills and time to moderate one.

Q **I'm interested in setting up a group like this. What is an ideal number of parents to get it off the ground?**

A *Research has shown that the best size for a support group is approximately eight to twelve members. But, as these things take time to gather momentum, please don't be disappointed if there are initially fewer attendees. It should build as word gets round, so don't give up.*

Q **How often should a group like this meet?**

A *There are no hard and fast rules; it is up to you. You could discuss this with the other members of the group at the first meeting and come to an agreement which suits all of you – and don't forget that it can be changed, of course.*

Q **My mind's gone blank. We'd like a good range of speakers – who could we invite?**

A *There are many possibilities; here are three to start you off. An enthusiastic teacher could share classroom management techniques, an occupational therapist might speak about techniques to improve motor skills and reduce clumsiness and a psychiatrist could do a question and answer session on medication.*

How did it go?

141

32

Let's play PlayStation

If the only activity your child can concentrate on is playing video games, don't despair. Finding out about the lesser known benefits of console games will offer some consolation.

There's new scientific evidence suggesting that video-game-based technology can improve attention span, decrease distractibility and increase children's ability to finish tasks.

Many children with ADHD can't concentrate at school, but have an uncanny ability to focus and concentrate on their video and computer games, achieving high scores and thrashing every competitor who comes their way.

To play a computer game well, children need good concentration, a level of forward planning, lateral thinking and sustained problem-solving abilities. A session on the Xbox or PlayStation could develop all of those skills. In addition, computer games can also teach children how social and scientific rules work. Impulsivity is a hallmark of ADHD; children often respond without thinking instead of taking stock of their options. Playing a computer game can help kids see what their options are.

Here's an idea for you...

Children with ADHD need a little direction to get the most out of playing computer games. Sit with your child while he's playing and encourage him to think about what he's doing when he wins a round or gets to the next level.

James Paul Gee, author of *What Video Games Have to Teach Us About Learning and Literacy*, has been so bold as to suggest that teachers can learn many useful lessons by looking at how these games draw players in and motivate them to concentrate and tackle complex problems. New York-based company Tabula Digita is making a 3D game to teach algebra, and the University of Wisconsin is making another to teach urban planning and the ecological, social, economic and cultural issues connected to it.

Many parents and teachers worry that computer games are bad news. However, research does seem to suggest the opposite at present. Children who regularly play computer games before going to school do better academically, particularly in maths. A study undertaken in Dundee by Derek Robertson of Learning and Teaching Scotland found that children who played the computer game called *More Brain Training from Dr Kawashima* daily for ten weeks showed improvements in both learning and behaviour. This game includes a series of number trials, reading tests, mathematical exercises and memory puzzles.

After the group of Dundee schoolchildren had played the game regularly for the ten weeks of the study, they all took a maths test – which they had also taken before the start of the project. All of them improved by at least 10% and one child even showed an improvement of 43%. In addition, the time for answering the papers was reduced from an average of seventeen minutes to just over thirteen. The study was conducted in other academic institutions with similar results.

What isn't clear is whether less obviously educational games would be as effective. American psychologist Henry Owen has developed a video game to improve his patients' attention. This particular one is designed to help kids with ADHD focus and concentrate. On the commercial level, apparently driving simulator games work best, and guts and gore games don't do any good at all, so you might do well to encourage your child to have a go at something like *Flight Simulator 3* rather than some of the other options. Finally, when choosing games, keep any you select well within your child's range of abilities so that they are supportive rather than discouraging. If he can achieve and win some of the lower levels of a game, he'll feel confident and be spurred on to bigger wins.

Try another idea...

Have a break from the console every now and then and spend some time reading together. **IDEA 50, *Reading improves vision*, explains why this is particularly important for kids with ADHD.**

Defining idea...

Games could play a part in integrating real use of abstract knowledge. Civilisation *is a good example; it teaches about material and geographical contingency in the progression of history.* Nintendo's Animal Crossing *is another – my five year old learned almost everything he ever needs to know about long-term debt by figuring out how to pay off his home mortgage in the game.*
IAN BOGOST, games designer and theorist

145

How did it go?

Q **My son's PlayStation seems to be the only thing that captures his attention for prolonged periods. He has several favourite games, but his father and I have recently wondered whether so-called 'edutainment' games might be better. What do you think?**

A *It sounds counterintuitive, but not necessarily. Many are poorly designed, nor are they particularly educational. Boring education programmes masquerading as games can be a major turn-off. Many commercial games can develop concentration, attention and problem-solving skills. Educational games can do this too, but many educationists and psychologists are wary of poorly designed ones. You're probably better off investing in an attractive commercial game your child will enjoy rather than hijacking what he perceives as his leisure time with educational games that may offer little advantage.*

Q **When our son plays up, we withdraw his Xbox. He seems to understand this and his behaviour invariably improves. If there are so many potential benefits to using it, should we be taking it away?**

A *Well, the key here is* potential *benefits. Research in this area is still rudimentary and treating the Xbox as a privilege that needs to be earned through good behaviour is a good principle. It sounds as if it is very motivating for him, so do continue to use it as a reward. Perhaps instead of withdrawing it, you could list the kind of behaviour that is desirable in your household and reward him with an extra half an hour on the Xbox each day he achieves it.*

146

33

Food for thought

If your child is only eating rubbish or rushes about at a rate that burns three times the energy she's taking in, it's time to address the culinary crisis.

You can contribute to your child's wellbeing by developing and enhancing innovative techniques to prevent or tackle eating problems in ADHD.

Children with ADHD who are very squirmy or run about a lot require more fuel, in the form of food, than quieter children. The paradox is that kids with ADHD often find it difficult to sit still through a meal, and leave the table or abandon their lunchbox before they have eaten much. To add insult to injury, the medication most commonly used to treat ADHD – stimulant medication – can stop children feeling hungry. If that seems to be the case with your child, see if you can plan meals around the time when the next dose is due, or when you notice the effect of the last dose wearing off. As hyperactivity increases, the chances are that hunger will too. You don't have to cook a three-course sit-down meal at the drop of a hat; a high-energy portable snack may be all you need in those circumstances.

Children who have lost their appetite often eat ordinary food if it is dressed up. For example, a pizza is more appealing if you make a face out of slices of pastrami and use pepper strips for a mouth.

Begin with breakfast. A traditional cooked breakfast before a morning dose of stimulant medication could be the vital difference between an adequate calorie intake and a malnourished child. If you can't stomach a fry-up every morning, a sausage sandwich, scrambled eggs on toast and a milkshake made with full fat milk would be just fantastic.

Use whole milk all the time if your child is light for his or her age. Pour it over cereals, offer it to drink with meals and use it in sauces. Buy full fat ice cream and yoghurts for your child too. Low fat is important for older children and adults, but for overactive, underweight youngsters, getting energy matters more.

If you don't already do this, introduce family meal times. Every evening, sit down together as a family and eat dinner. You might like to agree – as a family – that everyone has to stay at the table until the last person has finished. Children with ADHD can often be encouraged to stay at the dinner table if something captures their attention. Give yours a task like serving up, or play a children's audio book during dinner. If your child really can't manage to sit still, or your partner can't bear another audio rendition of Little Red Riding Hood, teach your child to ask to leave the table, rather than just skipping off. And remember grandma's rule: no dessert for those who haven't eaten a decent main course.

One cannot think well, love well, sleep well, if one has not dined well.
VIRGINIA WOOLF

Call a ceasefire in the battle of wills. It really doesn't matter if your child eats coco pops instead of muesli, or that she wants to eat them for dinner from time to time. Aim for a varied, balanced diet, be flexible and stay cool as a cucumber over her refusal to eat anything green. Red peppers may be the answer.

If your child takes a lunchbox to school, imagine her eating on the move, and choose food that can be picked up and eaten on the go: fresh fruit, samosas, flapjacks, strips of sweet pepper, small meringues, cucumber batons, four squares of chocolate, mini pepperoni, fairy cakes or wontons. Remember the drinks parties you went to before you had kids? The sort of hors d'oeuvres and nibbles served there are ideal. Felafel, salmon blinis and prawn vol-au-vents may be acquired tastes, so start sneaking them into lunch boxes early. The other secret to feeding children with ADHD is variety. Put grapes in your kid's lunchbox every day, and they'll turn into raisins. Instead, vary things: pear today, plum tomorrow. And get snacking. Small mid-morning and mid-afternoon snack breaks replenish energy levels and stop surges in blood sugar, which can make cranky children more even-tempered.

Try another idea...

Why not cook together using some new recipes from a library cookbook? Find out why making a regular visit to the local library can help in other ways too, in IDEA 50, *Reading improves vision.*

Defining idea...

One should eat to live, not live to eat.
CICERO

149

How did it go?

Q   My friends tell me that my daughter's hyperactivity may be caused by food allergies or reactions to artificial additives. There's so much confusing information out there about restrictive diets. What is the best sort of diet to help someone with ADHD?

A   *One of the biggest myths about ADHD is that it is exclusively caused by food allergies or intolerances. Sugar, artificial food colouring, preservatives, refined carbohydrates and dairy products are most frequently targeted, despite evidence to the contrary. The best diet for a child with ADHD is the same healthy diet for any other child: variety, five portions of fruit and vegetables every day, not too many unhealthy fats, watch the additives, get protein from a variety of sources, don't forget carbohydrates.*

Q   My nine-year-old daughter really struggles to use a knife and fork and I think she sometimes gives up on her food because it's too much effort. She can't eat finger food for the rest of her life, but she's getting skinny. What can I do?

A   *She's in good company. Lots of children with ADHD find using cutlery challenging at best and frustrating at worst. If she's tired at the end of the day, she will be more likely to give up easily. It's important she perseveres. Try this next time she gives up: congratulate her on managing to use her cutlery, cut up a few more mouthfuls for her and let her have a spoon for those. The deal is that you will help her out with the spoon, but only at the evening meal and only when she has tried with a knife and fork first.*

34
Giving consequences

When children have ADHD, their behaviour is a bit like the sea – always changing, flat and calm one minute, wild and crashing the next.

Sometimes you can see a storm on the horizon, at other times behaviour changes with little warning. You can learn how to influence this behaviour so it doesn't drown you.

Here is a set of principles that increase the chances of good behaviour happening again, and bad behaviour happening less often. These principles come from a school of psychology called behaviourism.

There are various forms of behavioural interventions used for children with ADHD. An example of very intensive behaviour therapy was used in the NIMH Multimodal Treatment Study of Children with ADHD, which involved a child's teacher, family and participation in an all-day, eight-week summer camp. The consulting therapist worked with teachers to develop behaviour management strategies that addressed behavioural problems interfering with classroom behaviour and academic performance. A trained classroom aide worked with a child for twelve weeks in the classroom, to provide support and reinforcement for appropriate, on-task behaviour.

Here's an idea for you...

When choosing reinforcers, it's really important to consider what is likely to motivate your child. Some children will be devastated to stay in and miss out on playing with their friends. Others will not be that bothered, and will enjoy being on the computer indoors just as much. Take ten minutes to brainstorm what would motivate your child and then think about ways you make them act as positive or negative reinforcers.

Parents met with the therapist alone and in small groups to learn approaches for handling problems at home and school. The summer day camp was aimed at improving social behaviour, academic work and sports skills. Clearly most people won't have access to anything like this level of expertise or intensive help, but you can learn and use some behavioural techniques easily.

Behaviourists use the term 'reinforce' to describe consequences to a behaviour that increase the chance that the behaviour will happen again. 'Punishments' are consequences that decrease the chance of that behaviour happening again. Behaviourists also refer to positive and negative consequences. Positive or negative don't mean good or bad in this context, but they refer to whether something is being added or removed. Using positive and negative reinforcers is called making a behavioural intervention. It's best to use a mixture of reinforcers and punishments to change behaviours, with a heavy emphasis on reinforcers and a lesser weight on punishments.

Here are some examples. Remember, reinforcements increase desirable behaviours and punishments decrease unwanted ones.

- **Adding something:** Positive reinforcement would mean something like giving a star to a child for sitting still at the dinner table (adding a star increases the odds of him sitting still again). Positive punishment would be making a teenager do extra chores for blurting out obscenities to his teacher (adding the chores decreases the odds that he will swear impulsively again).

IDEA 38, *Restorative justice: how to punish effectively*, explains how you can reduce unwanted behaviours.

Try another idea...

- ■ **Removing something:** Negative reinforcement would mean a child not having to go to bed at the usual time on Saturday night because he was good all day (removing his usual bedtime increases the odds that he will be good again next Saturday). Negative punishment would be keeping a child in for the evening after he has been caught lying about how much homework he has (removing the opportunity to play outside decreases the odds that he will lie again).

Another way to reduce behaviours you want to see the back of is to ignore them. For instance, your child swears and is abusive if he doesn't get his own way. If you ignore him, he will eventually stop doing this as it doesn't get any reaction. Ignoring – withdrawing your attention – is a type of negative reinforcement.

A common intervention for children with ADHD is a combination of approaches, sometimes using medication along with behavioural interventions. Using medication often creates a window of opportunity to allow you to help your child learn more effective behaviour.

The best way to behave is to misbehave.
MAE WEST

Defining idea...

How did it go?

Q **I recently started grounding my son for the next evening when he does something wrong. It worked really well for a while and his behaviour was good. Unfortunately, that change was rather short lived and he now seems to be behaving even worse than before. What's going on?**

A *You've come across something that behaviourists call the 'honeymoon period' and the 'extinction burst'. When you started your behavioural intervention, your son's behaviour improved. A sudden, almost miracle-like improvement is common – the honeymoon period. With many children with ADHD, this improvement is short lived and like you, many parents notice increases in misbehaviour. That's the extinction burst, and many parents become discouraged when it happens. This is the hardest time to be consistent and patient; it is as if your son is trying to demonstrate that he's going to continue to misbehave no matter what you do. The trick to getting over the extinction burst is to stick to your plan and keep reinforcing. It will work again if you hang in there.*

Q **My son finds it really hard to sit still for a meal, and I'd love to reinforce this with him getting fifteen minutes' extra computer time. He's up for the plan, and I think he really wants to achieve it, but he's just too squirmy and not getting the reinforcer is dragging us both down. I don't want to give it to him without him doing his bit. What do you recommend?**

A *I suggest you try a technique called 'shaping'. This means reinforcing the small steps that lead to the ultimate goal. So you could perhaps break the fifteen minutes of computer use into three five-minute slots, one to be earned for each course of the meal.*

35

Everyone's a winner

Playing games can develop confidence and self-esteem, both of which are likely to be lower in children with ADHD. So let the dice, and the good times, roll.

A lot of the time, parenting a child with ADHD can feel like drudgery. Making some time for play and spontaneous fun can make it less of a burden.

Play fosters feelings of warmth and closeness between parents and children with ADHD. By playing with your child, you can help develop attention, concentration, imagination, problem solving and communication skills. Children are more creative and have fewer behaviour problems if their parents spend time playing with them. Here are some suggestions.

ANIMAL MAGIC

Animal Magic is a great game for developing self-esteem. It reminds children what they are good at in an indirect and fun way. Kids with ADHD spend so much time hearing negative comments from adults and other children that they can sometimes forget what they do well. It goes like this:

Here's an idea for you...

Children with ADHD can find it especially hard to wait at airports. Turn a potentially excruciating wait into a fun game. For instance, if you are waiting at the airport to collect Aunt Maud from Honolulu, everyone waiting has to place a bet on how many people will come through the departure gate until Aunt Maud arrives. Whoever is closest wins, and can gloat to Aunt Maud. If you are waiting at a bus stop, you can vary this game by guessing how many red cars will pass before the bus stops.

■ 'If I were an animal I would be a _____. Because it's good at _____. Just like me.'

Here's an example:
■ 'If I were an animal I would be an elephant. Because it's good at remembering. Just like me.'
And another:
■ 'If I were an animal I would be a mule. Because mules are good at being strong and standing their ground. Just like me.'
This game can be good for getting rid of extra energy, too. Act out the animal and, as a variation, make the animal's sound and have other players guess what it is.

FROLF

Frolf is a combination of Frisbee and golf. My friend Mark put me onto this and it really is a super way for kids to burn off excess energy. You don't need any fancy equipment, just a Frisbee. The idea is that you choose a marker, like a tree or lamppost, which is the equivalent of a hole in golf. Each player then has to reach this landmark using the Frisbee, and aiming for the shortest number of tries. If your child has been cooped up in a classroom all day, a round of Frolf on the way home may be just the game.

MEMORY

Memory is a card game that is good for building concentration and attention. You need a set of cards in matching pairs (you could even make your own, with duplicate pictures, but the backs must all be identical). Place them all face down in a random way, not in straight lines or anything like that. Take it in turns with your child to turn two at a time over. Anyone who finds a matching pair wins those, and they are removed from the game. The winner is the person with the biggest pile of cards at the end.

Getting physical has more benefits than simply getting rid of extra energy. Find out why it's important for children with ADHD to be fit, In IDEA 4, *Move it*. In IDEA 5, *What's not wrong?*, you'll discover a game you can play with your child to encourage a positive mindset and find solutions to sticky situations.

Try another idea...

IF I WAS MY PET

Being able to see things from another perspective helps kids understand that there is more than one way to look at circumstances. If you have a pet, encourage your child to imagine what it is like being that pet. Where would be a good place to play? How would you get attention? How would you let people know you are hungry, tired or bored? Would it be fun to go for a walk? Or a ride in the car? If you don't have a pet, choose an animal in the garden like an ant or worm and do the same thing.

If you want to focus children's attention, you first have to capture their interest.
BARBARA SHER, occupational and play therapy specialist

Defining idea...

157

How did it go?

Q **Most evenings this week, I've tried to suggest a game, but my son just isn't interested. He'd rather just play computer games on his own. What can I do?**

A *Go with it. It sounds as if he is letting you know what he wants to do. Instead of trying to impose a game or activity, why not play computer games with him? Chances are his skills in this area may be a little ahead of yours, so he'll get a real boost showing you how to play. Once you have done this together a few times, he'll probably be more interested in playing other games with you too.*

Q **My daughter really loves Frolf and wants to play it every day. I'm really bored of it and want to get her into other things. What do you suggest?**

A *Oh dear. I'm sorry you're bored, but I'm afraid that's just how it is sometimes. Do you remember when she was a toddler and wanted the same story every night? This is just a variation. When it comes to play, kids rule. Resist the temptation to shoehorn her into other games. She is probably practising certain new skills over and over to become really proficient at them. Pushing her may make her feel incompetent, so is best avoided. Respecting her pace will help her develop her concentration span.*

36

Intermittent reinforcement

If you're tearing your hair out because of your child's shocking behaviour, a lesson from gambling could be invaluable.

Slot machines and soft drink vending machines both take your hard-earned cash, but deliver vastly different rewards. There's a lesson in this, and it could change your child's behaviour.

One of the commonest ways your child's behaviour is reinforced is by intermittent reinforcement. By this I mean that your child's behaviour is reinforced or rewarded only some of the time when it is displayed. Because kids learn not to expect their behaviour to get the desired response every time, they learn to be persistent – and problem behaviours can be maintained for a long time.

For example, imagine you put a coin into a vending machine to buy a can of coke. If no can of coke was dispensed, you'd most likely feel annoyed, and rightly so. If you were very thirsty, you might put in another coin, but if you still didn't get a drink,

Here's an idea for you...

Think back over the behaviours your child has that are troublesome and see if you can identify any times when you may have inadvertently been reinforcing them. Once you've identified those times, brainstorm alternative things you might do when you are feeling like giving in, write them down and keep the list handy for crisis times.

you'd be forgiven for giving the machine a shake or kick and not wasting any more money. If there was a phone number on the machine, you might call and complain.

Now imagine you put a coin into a slot machine in a fairground. If you didn't get any money back, you might well part with a few more coins. This is because you never expected it to work the first time. One of the reasons people get hooked on slot machines is because they win just often enough to make them want to keep playing and trying for a win.

This principle, intermittent reinforcement, can help explain why some behaviours in your ADHD child continue, even when you feel you have been very careful not to reinforce them. It also explains why activities like fishing can be so much fun: you never know when you are going to get a bite.

Say, for instance, that you want your child to do her homework before watching television. She might find this a real struggle, and nag and pester you right through her homework to let her just watch a bit of television. If you hold your ground almost every evening, but then one day have a bad day at work, come home feeling tense and give in to these demands, then that is enough to teach her that nagging is worth it – sometimes it works.

The key to modifying your child's behaviour is working out what is reinforcing it. When you're trying to work this out, picture the slot machines and the vending machine and ask yourself honestly if you have been a little like a slot machine in occasionally reinforcing behaviour.

You can find out more about reinforcers and how best to use them in IDEA 34, *Giving consequences.*

Try another idea...

Intermittent reinforcement explains why some people get hooked on gambling; it is the thrill of not knowing whether you will win. If you never won or always won it would be impossible to become a gambler. The fact that intermittent recognition works so well that it can form a powerful habit like gambling is actually good news for parents of children with ADHD. It means you can use intermittent reinforcement to your advantage. You don't have to be perfect at remembering to reward good behaviour every single time it occurs. Every now and again may even be more effective. In fact, once the desired behaviour has occurred consistently or a few weeks with continuous reinforcement from you, it is probably going to be better if you switch to intermittent reinforcement.

The typical gambler might not really understand the probabilistic nuances of the wheel or the dice, but such things seem a bit more tractable than, say, trying to raise a child in this lunatic society of ours.
ARTHUR S. REBER, *The New Gambler's Bible*

Defining idea...

How did it go?

Q **Our son has ADHD and we suspect that certain additives make his behaviour worse, so we eliminate them as far as possible from his diet. He likes certain sweets which contain these additives, and every now and then I feel sorry for him and let him have one. My husband thinks this is a type of intermittent reinforcement and that I should stop giving in. I think that the occasional treat is important. What's your view?**

A *It all depends on the context. If your son is pestering for sweets that you don't want him to eat as they have adverse effects on his behaviour, and you are giving in to his demands, then your husband is right. The problem with this would be that you are teaching your son to keep asking for the sweets – next time might be the time he gets away with having them. On the other hand, if you are using the sweets to treat him as a reward for good behaviour, this is not the same as giving in and relenting. I suspect that part of the tension between you and your husband is over the additives, additives that you suspect make your son's behaviour worse. Might I suggest you substitute additive-free sweets and agree as a family under what circumstances your son can have them?*

Q **I've read elsewhere that children with ADHD need continuous reinforcement and much more reinforcement for good behaviour than other kids. Does intermittent reinforcement really work for them?**

A *This is a good question. You are right that children with ADHD need both more immediate consequences and more frequent consequences for behaviour than children who do not have it. However, once you have done frequent, consistent reinforcing and have the results you were looking for, switching to intermittent reinforcement is a good ploy.*

37

Memory gym

Poor short-term memory affects reading, maths, exam performance and causes no end of daily hassles from forgotten lunchboxes to missed homework.

I've even met mothers who asked for their children's hearing to be tested. They were convinced their kids must be deaf as they seemed so unaware of what was going on...

ADHD has a catastrophic effect on short-term memory. Children may remember a birthday party a couple of years ago in almost photographic detail, yet manage to forget instructions from a teacher in seconds.

Children with ADHD usually have good long-term memories but poor short-term – or working – memory. These short-term memory problems mean that children underperform at school, especially in tests. Instructions are forgotten, messages are half heard. That's why they can be terrible at remembering those instructions and are unable to remember significant components of lessons. It can be a particular problem when information is given in a sequence, as children with ADHD have trouble with sequences too.

Once children are old enough to have mobile phones, use text messaging to remind them to do something, like taking medication or returning books to the library. It is an unobtrusive way of keeping in contact. Agree with them first that you are going to do this, so it does not feel intrusive.

There are seven things you can do which will either help develop short-term memory skills, or help your child work round poor short-term memory.

■ **Rhymes.** These are a great way of remembering complex information. There are two rules for rhymes. The ones kids make up themselves are most likely to be remembered, and the ruder the better.

■ **Mnemonics.** The rude rule applies to mnemonics too. Fifteen-year-old Frank has ADHD and told me he uses the mnemonic 'ARSE' to remind him of the sequence for working with his classroom aide. A stands for getting the aide's **A**ttention, R is for making a **R**equest, S is for waiting for him to **S**ay something and E is to remind him to **E**xplain what he's understood. It sounds terribly irreverent, but has transformed a chaotic classroom experience into one that is fruitful and productive.

The mind is not a vessel to be filled, but a fire to be ignited.
PLUTARCH

■ **Association.** Most people learn well by association. If each piece of new information is associated with something which is already known, kids with ADHD have a much better chance of retaining it. They can make the most of association when they are revising for tests, by learning facts in the room they will be examined in, if possible.

■ **Visual cues.** Children with ADHD often have better visual skills than children who don't, so use this to your advantage. List all the facts that your child needs to remember, for instance what to take on a school trip or a list of revision for a test, and help her make a visual picture that includes all the main concepts. It tends to work best if the picture is bizarre and wacky. Practise next time you go food shopping together. Make a picture of the shopping list in your heads. It might be a loaf of bread, wrapped in tin foil and smothered in tomato ketchup, then floating in milk. See how many items she remembers and encourage her to use this in other situations. You can help your child improve her memory by using a wider range of visual cues, too. Put a weekly planner somewhere visible, and write or draw prompts on it.

■ **Writing on hands.** Yes, it looks unsightly, but many children can be kept on track by writing important information like a parent's phone number on the back of one hand. Notes in pockets are going to get lost, hands are hopefully going to stay attached.

■ **Lists.** Encourage your child to make a list of key facts when revising. Get her to read a chapter and summarise it into ten key words in a list. Each word will act as a trigger for more information.

■ **Step by step instructions.** This is one for teachers and parents. Long, complicated instructions and sequences don't work for children with ADHD. Each task needs to be chunked up and instructions given one at a time. This way there's a much higher chance those instructions will be remembered and followed.

> **Most kids with poor short-term memory also have difficulty with time management. IDEA 27, *Every second counts*, is perfect for those with memory problems.**

Try another idea...

How did
it go?

Q **My son's teacher says his memory is basically all right, but his attention is the problem – his poor attention stops him holding on to instructions and other information. I don't know if she's right. What can we do?**

A   *This is a tricky one. Poor attention is part of ADHD and is possibly affecting your son's performance in school. Inattention means children are more likely to rush through work without checking it, and make silly errors. It also means it is difficult for children to pick up on key parts of a message as they may be distracted by irrelevancies. Both these aspects of attention are closely linked to memory, and it is slightly artificial to tease them apart, or to say with confidence that a child does not have a memory difficulty. Put simply, if he can't attend to what is going on in class, he isn't going to be able to remember it. A lot of the ruses in this idea address both memory and attention, so I wouldn't worry too much about what the root cause is and would focus instead on solutions.*

Q **My teenage son is virtually dependent on lists and memory jogs. If it isn't written down or stored in his PDA, he's lost. It's almost obsessive. How can we wean him off them?**

A   *If it works, why worry? Many adults are reliant on lists and most successful business people have an organised PA who keeps the show on the road. For the record, I'm pretty reliant on lists too. If it ain't broke...*

38

Restorative justice: how to punish effectively

When children with ADHD do something wrong, you sometimes need to decrease that behaviour effectively, using appropriate punishment. Here's how.

When psychologists and psychiatrists talk about punishment, they don't mean locking children in a dark cellar or grounding them until it's time to go to university...

Put simply, a punishment is a consequence that leads to a reduction in bad behaviour. It tells your child with ADHD what you do and don't want them to do. Many behaviours have natural consequences. Natural consequences are things that happen in response to your child's behaviour without anyone else getting involved. For instance, if a child with ADHD forgets to bring his bike inside, one possible natural consequence is that it will get stolen, and this will be so awful that it will decrease the likelihood of him leaving a bike outside again.

Natural consequences are an excellent alternative to punishment. Children learn and change their behaviour after experiencing consequences. The trouble is that natural consequences don't always get rid of the behaviour that you'd like to see

Here's an idea for you...

If your child is doing something that you'd like to change and there isn't a natural consequence, establish some clear and fair ground rules. Let him know what will happen if he breaks the rules and when this happens, implement the specific, time-limited punishment to deter his action in future.

the back of. For instance, if your child hasn't revised for a test, cheats and then gets away with it, cheating has led to him excelling in a test he would otherwise have flunked. There are also many behaviours that don't have natural consequences. For instance, if your son dawdles on the way home from school and misses the bus, you may be out of your mind with worry about where he is, but he might be oblivious to that – and so there's no natural consequence to his poor organisation.

Effective punishment is an action used to decrease behaviours that don't have natural consequences, or when the natural consequence is unlikely to reduce the unwanted behaviour. It's important to realise that punishment alone won't teach your child new behaviour, but applied effectively ought to get rid of problematic behaviour. Before you can give effective punishments, you need to take three steps:

- Be clear about ground rules with your child. The rules should be fair, easy to follow and enforceable.
- When your child breaks a rule, be calm and direct, and apply the planned punishment effectively.

Defining idea...

The liar's punishment is not in the least that he is not believed, but that he cannot believe anyone else.
GEORGE BERNARD SHAW

168

■ When selecting a punishment, remember that it ought to fit the crime. Check that it has these three key features: is specific to the misdemeanour (if you are late home, you lose the chance to play out tomorrow), is time limited (the child loses the chance to play out tomorrow, not for the next month) and is appropriate (no sackcloth or ashes involved).

Kids with ADHD are less likely to learn what is acceptable behaviour if adults around them react in different ways. IDEA 12, *Home uniform*, is all about being predictable and consistent in different settings.

Try another idea...

Many parents and teachers get into a rut with punishment because they end up doling out punishments that are ineffective and don't help children with ADHD change their behaviours. Punishments are ineffective when they lack any of the three key features above. So, if a punishment is not specific, time limited or doesn't fit the crime, it won't work. If a boy with ADHD comes home late from school and his parents ground him until the end of term, take away his computer and nag him every day about it, he's going to feel dreadful but won't be effectively punished, so it won't lead to a change in his behaviour.

Remember that punishments will be ineffective if they are:
■ Threatened but not carried out
■ Given in anger or in response to a crisis
■ Given reactively
■ Given inconsistently
■ Not specific to the crime

Punishment: the justice that the guilty deal out to those who are caught.
ELBERT HUBBARD, American writer

Defining idea...

How did
it go?

Q   **My daughter has ADHD and creates some sort of scene every morning if she doesn't get her own way. The trouble is, punishments just don't touch her. I tell her every day that if we are late, she will have to have a punishment, but she doesn't look bothered. It really stresses me out because I run my own business and am able to manage a staff team, but can't get my daughter under control. What can I do?**

A   *I think the answer is in your question. You need to do something, and not just tell her you are going to do something. When children get lots of threats but hardly any consequences, they are just not motivated to change their behaviour. Say an employee of yours left work early every day, and each day you threatened to fire him if he persisted but never took any action, there'd be no incentive for him to change. You've clearly got some great people-management skills at work. It's time to stop talking and start acting at home too.*

Q   **I was brought up in a strict, religious home and when we did something wrong we were spanked. Don't you agree this is a good, quick, time-limited way to deal with unwanted behaviour?**

A   *I don't think there is ever a place for hitting children. Violence is never an effective or fair punishment, and spanking often happens in anger, when parents are losing control. There are many better ways, ways that are non-verbal – like withdrawing privileges – and these should be your options of choice.*

39

Problem solving

Children with ADHD are impulsive and may hit, kick, punch or push when faced with conflict, as it's the first response that pops into their head.

Children act impulsively because they lack good strategies for solving problems. Teach them to generate solutions to problems and help them plan ahead.

Many children with ADHD have a limited range of ways of responding to conflict and do the first thing that comes into their minds. Some seem to always be in trouble for hitting out or getting into fights. It might be because they are impulsively reacting in an aggressive way. They can't think of how to respond when they feel hurt or frustrated, so they hit, punch, kick or throw something. You can teach them how to identify and weigh up other ways of responding, however.

An effective four-stage problem solving-strategy has been developed by Professor of Special Education Carolyn Hughes, and works well:
- Identify the problem.
- Select a course of action.
- Implement a solution.
- Evaluate the solution.

You can guide your child through each stage.

Children learn problem solving through modelling, by watching how adults solve problems and imitating them. Next time you are facing a challenge, think how you present it in front of your child. Do you impulsively leap on the first solution, or do you demonstrate a more structured problem-solving approach? Take as many opportunities as you can to show how to solve problems. Your actions really will speak louder than words.

IDENTIFY AND DEFINE THE PROBLEM

Professor Hughes suggests you can help your child define the problem by asking these questions:

- What do you want?
- What do you have now?
- What's the gap between what you want and what you have?

Children under twelve will probably struggle with the third one, so you can help them by explaining how you see the gap. Once you have agreed, make a note together of the gap between what your child wants and what your child has. This statement ought to define the problem. For instance: 'You want to play with people and not bite them. At the moment you play with people but when you get cross you bite. The gap between what you want and what you have is that you can play with people nicely, but bite them when you are cross. You need to find a way to play with people and not bite them.'

SELECT A COURSE OF ACTION

Next, look at potential solutions. There are a number of ways of generating this list:
- Select a solution from a list of options. Unfortunately, not every problem comes with a list of potential solutions. Even when there is one, each would need to be examined to determine the pros and cons.

- Pick a solution that sounds like it would work. This method is easy because it does not require any previous knowledge. However, there is no way to know whether such a solution will actually work.

- Use an analogy from a similar situation. This can be a quick starting point for developing a solution but analogies are not always relevant and the solutions may not be feasible.

- Brainstorm to generate a number of potential solutions to the problem. This method of identifying a course of action can be interesting and fun. Once you have got a list of possible solutions:
  - Identify the pros and cons of each. Do this by asking, 'what do you think might happen if you did that?'
  - Think about what's needed for each option.
  - Consider all possible costs and risks for each.
  - Review each option and select the one that seems to fit best.

Children who have difficulty controlling rages and aggressive outbursts may need to work on their anger. IDEA 2, *Cross words*, will help.

Try another idea...

We can't solve problems by using the same kind of thinking we used when we created them.
ALBERT EINSTEIN

Defining idea...

IMPLEMENT THE SOLUTION

Now it's time for action. To help children implement the solution smoothly, make sure they:

- Know the solution. Can your kid talk about what he is going to do? You might need to role play and have a trial run.
- Have the skills necessary to do the things described. If his preferred solution is not biting other children but challenging them to a game of chess, it won't work if he can only play snakes and ladders. Seriously, if he needs new skills, make sure there is a realistic time frame available for acquiring them.
- Decide when and how to implement the new solution. The start of term? The start of next week? This afternoon at rugby practice?

EVALUATION

If the stages have been followed, the chances are that the new solution worked well. If it didn't go quite to plan, it's time for a brief review. Start at the first stage, and work through them again. A common sticking point is not defining the problem accurately, or being lax about deadlines.

Q **We're not getting very far with brainstorming. Can you give us some tips?**

A *Of course. When brainstorming, give children the freedom to say anything they like, however silly or impractical. After each suggestion, say something like, 'yes, you could do that, and what else might you try? What else might work?' This helps them generate as long a list as possible. And don't forget to write your ideas down, either.*

Q **My thirteen-year-old son has used the strategy well for avoiding playground fights, and we have since tried it to solve the problems of him being disorganised with homework. He has brainstormed and come up with good ideas, but finds it hard to put them into practice. How can he make the last step?**

A *It's great that your son's been able to identify problems and work out a solution – he's just not able to implement it this time. Prompting from you could feel like nagging, so get him to try other reminders like a note on the calendar or an alarm on his phone. Some kids find picking a specific day to start a new solution and marking it on the calendar works well.*

How did it go?

40

When... then...

It's easy to get into power struggles with children who have ADHD. They are easily frustrated if they don't get their own way. This is a strategy for power-struggle management.

Use the 'when/then' rule for kids with ADHD instead of nagging them when their impulsivity and poor concentration cause them to forget things.

Don't get into battles with your child with ADHD, but use the when/then rule. This rule helps you encourage your child to do something that he or she does not want to do, or forgets to do. For instance, say she finds it hard to finish her homework. There's always a bit left undone, or a vital book left at school or instructions misplaced so she doesn't know what her homework is. This leads to arguments at home, detentions in school and lots of misery and frustration all round. She loves skateboarding, so you can broker a deal: '**when** all your homework is done, **then** you can go to the skate park'. Result? Her marks improve, she's more focused on homework and her skateboarding is improving too.

The when/then rule works best when you use it every day. Next time you find yourself in a situation that feels challenging or exasperating, see if you can turn a command or complaint into a when/then sentence. Deliver it in as calm a voice as you can muster, and see what happens.

Or say your son throws his coat on the floor every day when he gets in from school and races into the lounge to switch the television on. You are fed up with seeing his coat on the floor and have been reminding him, to no avail. There's a big argument, with door slamming and tears, almost every day. These can stop if you start using the when/then rule: '**when** you hang your coat up, **then** you may watch television'. At first your son – who has become used to his mother shouting – would be startled by your calm attitude and unsure about what was going on. He will then hang his coat up, switch on the television and – three weeks on – doesn't need reminding.

You can use the when/then rule in lots of other situations too; for example, 'when you've cleaned your shoes, you may play outside'. Think of some times when you might like to use when/then... 'When your hair is brushed, then you can come down for dinner'; 'When you've had a bath and are ready for bed, then we can read a story together.' Use it as an alternative to saying no or nagging. Children with ADHD often struggle with correct sequencing, or with the order of a task. This teaches them to set priorities.

When you are using this technique, always use the words 'when' and 'then'. They are magic words:

■ 'When you clean your teeth, then we can go to granny's.'

■ 'When you finish your dinner, then we can go to the cinema.'

Make sure your child has your full attention before giving a when/then command. Make eye contact and be prepared to get down to floor level to do this. It shows you mean business and captures the most fleeting attention for long enough for you to give a succinct when/then. Use a neutral tone of voice. Change your tone from, 'How can you even think of watching television when your mother is struggling with all the dishes?' to the more neutral (and kinder), 'when the dishes are done, then we'll watch *The Simpsons* together.' If you sound too strict or grumpy, it doesn't work as well. There's something about bossy voices that bring out the rebel in many kids – and many adults.

Try another idea...

We all have bad days. If you forget to use the when/then rule and end up shouting instead, there's no need to beat yourself up over it. Check out IDEA 23, *Forgiven, not forgotten*, to discover why being harsh on yourself isn't a good strategy.

Defining idea...

People's behaviour makes sense if you think about it in terms of their goals, needs and motives.
THOMAS MANN

179

How did it go?

Q **I've used this and found it helpful, but it's difficult to find times to use it every day. My daughter is very impulsive and wilful, and does things like having a screaming fit in the supermarket if I won't buy her a chocolate bar. How could I make a when/then sentence work in a situation like that?**

A   *When/then works by encouraging good behaviour. If there isn't much good behaviour to encourage, you'll need to discourage bad behaviour by using a variant of when/then, called if/then. To use your supermarket example, you might say something like, 'I have said I'm not going to buy any chocolate today. If you keep asking me, then there will be no video this evening'.*

Q **My teenage son has ADHD and I'd like to try this with him as we're both fed up with me nagging all the time. I'm not short of finding 'whens', it's the 'thens' I struggle with. It's hard to know what might be appropriate. What can you suggest?**

A   *When/then works well at all ages, and it's great you've made a commitment to stop nagging. Apart from being tiring and sounding ugly, it doesn't work. My first suggestion is that you ask your son what would motivate him. These 'thens' are not rewards, they are the sorts of things children and young people would like to do, whereas 'whens' are other things they also have to do, but typically dislike doing. If your son doesn't have many interests, and isn't able to help you, try suggesting extra time on the computer, bedtime half an hour later or having a friend stay overnight.*

41

Growing pains

All grown up and ready to take on the world? Teen years are challenging for many children. For children with ADHD these years can be particularly hard.

All those problems — peer pressure, bullying, fear of failure, difficulty with friendships — are especially tough if you have ADHD. Here's how to make sure your teenager has an easier time.

All teenagers want to be independent, to enjoy freedom and do things for themselves. You don't need me to tell you that impulsive teenagers are more likely to experiment with alcohol, other drugs and sex without thinking through the consequences, and are more likely to break adult rules on a whim. There are some invigorating options for all those times parents resort to the unsuccessful extremes of retribution and tolerance. So here are five tips for easing growing pains for teens with ADHD.

CHOICES

Adults are in an ideal position to help teenagers make choices and experiment with better ones. Many teenagers with ADHD get into trouble because they follow the first option that pops into their head, without stopping to think of other options or

Here's an idea for you...

Encourage your teenager to organise his life by using some attractive stationery. Suggest a large calendar hung where it will be seen in the morning, funky diaries and notebooks, a brightly coloured pad for making lists, sticky reminder notes – and consider buying a special box for keys and the paperwork of daily life.

the consequences of following each impulse. Next time your teen is in trouble, take some time together to brainstorm alternative courses of action he might have followed, or things he could have said differently.

DELEGATION

Time to hand over some responsibility. For example, if your teenager is on medication, give him responsibility for taking it. Make a chart listing household rules and put it somewhere prominent like on the fridge. A second chart of household chores with space to check off a chore once it is done is useful too.

STRAIGHT TALKING

This is essential. Now, more than ever, home and school rules need to be straightforward and easily understood. Speak to your teenager and explain why you have particular rules, and consider which ones are truly important to you, and which ones are no longer necessary now he is older. It is particularly helpful for teenagers to understand reasons for each rule. When a rule is set, be clear about why.

CARS...

Most kids show an interest in driving from at least their mid-teens. In some countries, a learner's licence is available at fifteen and a driver's licence at sixteen. Statistics show that teenage drivers have more accidents per driving kilometre than any other age, and 20% of those who died in speed-related crashes were aged between fifteen and nineteen. Teenagers with ADHD, in their first two to five years of driving, have nearly four times as many car accidents, are more likely to cause injury in accidents, and have three times as many speeding records as young drivers without ADHD. I'm not saying this to scaremonger, as it is important for young people to become independent and driving is often a big part of that, but it is also important to be aware of the increased risks. Consider optimising stimulant medication before buying a set of wheels.

IDEA 24, *Getting homework done*, is written for older children and teens. Impulsiveness can get a lot of lippy teens into trouble; check out IDEA 2, *Cross words*, for some hints on anger management.

Try another idea...

A LITTLE ENCOURAGEMENT

Encourage the behaviour you want to see from your teenager. You don't need to wait for misbehaviour to cue you in to encourage him. Any time he helps around the house, co-operates or makes a positive contribution to family life, give an encouraging message. The more you encourage, the greater the likelihood that the good behaviour will continue.

Remember that you are in charge of what happens in your home. If your child is a typical teenager, he'll push the boundaries from time to time. You can always use time out – it can still work with teenagers. They can decide when they go to a time out area to calm down.

If I'd observed all the rules, I'd never have gotten anywhere.
MARILYN MONROE

Defining idea...

183

How did it go?

Q **I don't know what to do when my thirteen-year-old son refuses to do something and then blames his ADHD. He says things like 'I can't do my chores because I can't concentrate long enough'. His brothers, who don't have ADHD, do their chores, so it doesn't seem right for him not to. Can you help?**

A *This sort of comment and behaviour is aggressive and you're absolutely right that he ought to contribute to family life and not blame his ADHD. Give him a choice. Tell him he can either do his chores like everyone else, or he can pay for a cleaner out of his pocket money. Give him a couple of hours to think it over and offer to work with him to improve his concentration so that he can be part of the family. If he opts for the cleaner, he has learnt a lesson about responsibility – and budgeting.*

Q **My daughter has started storming out of the room whenever we have a minor disagreement. She slams doors and yells and screams. She's always been quite impulsive, but she really seems to be struggling to control herself and I'm not sure how to respond to her. What do you suggest?**

A *She might be letting out some pent-up frustrated feelings, or laying it on with a trowel for your benefit. The best way to respond is by not giving in to demands made when yelling or door slamming. These strops will pass. I'm afraid it's a case of sitting them out and not doing the most tempting thing, responding with pressure or homilies.*

42

Music to the ears

Playing music may help children with attention problems. Learning an instrument could also help focus the mind and develop attention skills.

There is some evidence suggesting that music might help with certain brain functions, which could benefit kids with ADHD.

For all their squirminess, children with ADHD have a propensity to hyperfocus on something and not give up until they are satisfied they can do no better. When this happens, they may be completely unmindful to what is going on around them. They can also be perfectionists when something really grabs them, which can be a real attribute when studying something like music.

There is some evidence to suggest that students with ADHD can excel at music, as they can possess this ability to totally focus on something (like a piece of music) if it really interests them. One example is the pop musician Daniel Bedingfield, who says he was inspired to write his chart hits by his childhood condition. When he was a child, Daniel was diagnosed with ADHD and was given appropriate treatment. Now in his twenties, Daniel feels that some aspects of his ADHD have actually been helpful to his song writing.

Here's an idea for you...

Learning an instrument may be a great way for children with ADHD to develop greater self-esteem. If your son or daughter has shown any interest or aptitude, it is worth choosing a teacher who has experience of children with attention and concentration difficulties, so that it doesn't become a self-defeating experience. By selecting a teacher with appropriate skills and expertise, you can help to set your child up to succeed and provide an experience of learning not always available in conventional classrooms.

Defining idea...

There is no feeling, except the extremes of fear and grief, that does not find relief in music.
GEORGE ELIOT, *The Mill on the Floss*

Music, even just listening to it, is often very important for kids with ADHD. Some psychologists have experimented with using music with children who have ADHD to help them to control their behaviour and focus on their learning. Two clear examples are playing quiet classical music for quiet independent activities, and lively, bouncy jazz for group work, but there are others. It is possible that some students may have learnt to associate the use of music with the various methods of their learning when they were children.

In 1993, the name 'The Mozart Effect' was the name given to psychologists' discoveries, when it was first shown that playing Mozart to people in an experiment increased their spatial-temporal reasoning. Spatial-temporal reasoning is the ability to visualise spatial patterns and mentally manipulate them. Almost all of us use it regularly – it's the skill we use when we are parallel parking, for instance.

Researchers at Brigham Young university found that when a group of children with ADHD listened to three forty-minute recordings of classical music a week, their brain waves moved to higher levels. This allowed them to focus much more on tasks while they listened. They claim that 70% continued to show improvement from regular music sessions six months later.

You might want to hear more about this topic from a music teacher or educational psychologist. A parent support group is a great forum for this. Find out more in IDEA 31, *Get in a gang.*

Try another idea...

Don Campbell, author of *The Mozart Effect*, says that listening to Mozart helps the mind organise time and space. He also claims that the many other benefits include:

- The ability to study for longer periods of time.
- Better test scores.
- Shorter learning times.
- Calmer hyperactive children and adults.
- Reduced levels of errors.
- Improved creativity and clarity.

It is controversial, and there is no conclusive, definite scientific proof either way, but listening to music is certainly not harmful and the claims are certainly worth looking at. With all this potential, it's got to be worth giving it a go.

Ah, music. A magic beyond all we do here!
J. K. ROWLING, *Harry Potter and the Philosopher's Stone*, 1997

Defining idea...

187

How did it go?

Q   **My son enjoys music and we thought it would be good for him to learn an instrument. He chose the violin but just hasn't got the concentration and focus needed to practise for the required half hour every day. He has the concentration span of the proverbial gnat and it just leads to frustrating scenes. What can we do?**

A   *I think it's a great idea that you're helping him pursue an interest like this. May I recommend that you lower your expectations? I think it is unrealistic for him to concentrate for half an hour in one go, so why not chunk this up? Aiming for five or six sessions of five-minute practices during the day is much more like it. These little amounts accrue, and as he makes progress he will be more likely to stick to his practice for six or seven minutes, building up to the full half hour. Many music lessons are an hour long, which is also likely to be too much for a kid with ADHD. Speak to his violin teacher about the ADHD and see if she would be amenable to a twenty-minute or half-hour lesson instead.*

Q   **We play Mozart to my fifteen-year-old to try to help him concentrate on his homework but he says it drives him up the wall. If he had his way, he'd listen to death metal. What can we do?**

A   *Let him listen to death metal. He's fifteen, and enforced Mozart is not going to make either him or you happy. The theory that classical music helps concentration is exactly that, just a theory.*

43

Learning from 'the Squirmies'

Taking a playful approach may be the best way to get serious with ADHD. Maintaining a sense of humour is half the battle against bad behaviour.

It may not feel like a laughing matter, but giving your child's ADHD a jokey name like 'the Squirmies' could end the behaviours that have adults close to tears in frustration.

In their book, *Playful Approaches to Serious Problems*, Jennifer Freeman, David Epston and Dean Lobovits describe Dean's meeting with a nine-year-old boy, Leon. These three therapists believe in bringing children's own creative solutions to the fore, by using light-hearted techniques.

Like many families where a child has ADHD, Leon's family were exasperated by his lack of self-control. He distracted others in class and was in trouble frequently. Dean gave Leon's hyperactivity the name 'the Squirmies' and helped Dean and his family make a list of behaviours that were unacceptable to Leon in terms of their effect on his friendships and school life. It transpired that Leon had a particular talent for

Here's an idea for you...

Blame and shame about ADHD can have a paralysing effect. Next time you speak to your child, try externalising ADHD in your language. For instance, instead of saying, 'what did you do to make all your friends go away?', try 'how is the [nickname] getting in the way of you playing with your friends?'

making up games. He enjoyed inventing them and had an active imagination. Dean asked Leon if he had ever used his talent for making up games to try to outwit the Squirmies so they didn't keep embarrassing him. Leon rose to the challenge and had decided to take aim at the Squirmies. It worked like this. He drew himself in the classroom. There were concentric circles starting from the limits of the classroom to the playground. If the Squirmies 'got' Leon in the classroom, they got ten points and Leon got zero, but if Leon held the Squirmies off by using calming techniques, he got more and more points for putting the Squirmies where they belonged – in the playground. Leon was on to a winner.

I'm sure you'll agree this is an elegant solution. Not every child will make up games in the way Leon did, but there are many things you can try with your child that use this technique. Giving the disorder a name like Squirmies is called 'externalising'.

Externalising was first introduced by narrative family therapists in the 1980s. When ADHD is externalised, it also becomes possible to identify practices that keep unwanted behaviour going, and then work to diminish them. The aim of externalising practices is to enable children to realise that they and their ADHD are *not* the same. Separating young people from problems is a great way to motivate kids with ADHD to face their responsibilities and rise to challenges.

Here are two things you can do immediately to start externalising ADHD:
- View it and speak to your child about it as a medical illness
- Get your child to give it a nickname

Once ADHD has a nickname and character, you can playfully start to explore your family's relationship with it. How old is it? How long has it been in your household? What can you do that keeps it outside? It also helps you make an important distinction – between a child who has been reduced to being described as 'hyperactive' to a child who has a monster called ADHD that you are all learning to tame.

Drawing ADHD can help give it an identity to fight and conquer. IDEA 49, *Drawing together*, explains the other benefits of getting creative.

Try another idea...

Here are some questions you might like to ask, once ADHD has a nickname:
- How does the [nickname] leave you feeling?
- Does it get in the way of making friends?
- Does it get you into trouble at school?
- Does it mess up how you get on at home?
- Has it being trying to wreck your chances of going to camp?

These are just a few of the sorts of questions you might like to ask. As you find answers, the chances are that you're also in for a few surprises. ADHD is never 100% successful in taking over your child's life, and you will see strengths shining through. Once you do identify a strength, stay playful, asking questions like:
- Where did the strength come from?
- What does it look like?
- What could we call it?
- How does it fight the [nickname]?

The problem is the problem, the person is not the problem.
Often-quoted maxim of narrative therapy

Defining idea...

191

How did it go?

Q   **I've got to admit I'm a bit confused. We've been understanding ADHD as a problem in my son's brain, which is part of him. Now you're asking us to act as if ADHD *isn't* part of him. How can it be part of him and not part of him at the same time?**

A   *I'm sorry to muddle you. You're quite right in thinking most experts now believe that ADHD arises due to a problem with the frontal lobe. It is also true that ADHD is approached here as if it were external to the person. The key is 'as if'. It's possible – and indeed desirable – to have this explanation in mind, and still be playful and give the problem this brain illness causes a fun name. This helps your child feel it's something they can master and conquer, rather than being a slave to.*

Q   **We're finding it really hard to come up with a nickname for my son's ADHD. Any suggestions?**

A   *Bet I've heard more nicknames than you've had hot dinners. Seriously, the best nickname will be one he comes up with himself. If he's struggling, ask him to draw the ADHD as an animal. This will give an indication of how he perceives it. Once he's done that you could get him to draw himself as the animal he most needs to be to fight it and win.*

44

School's out

The school called. There's big trouble. Fear not, this recovery plan will have your child back in their good books in no time.

This six-step programme is all about helping teachers maximise your child's potential.

STEP 1

Meeting your child's teacher early is one of the most powerful things you can do. Lots of children with ADHD face challenges at school. Distractibility and hyperactivity make it hard to focus and attend to work or to what the teacher is saying. Many children with ADHD struggle with organising their work, and staying on task. And because they are impulsive, they are more likely to get into trouble, as they don't always think through the consequences of their actions. Harnessing a teacher's ideas and experience can propel your child towards new heights at school. Ask about an Individual Educational Plan (IEP) for your child and make sure the special educational needs co-ordinator knows you both, as well.

STEP 2

Teach the teachers. From time to time, children with ADHD can become classroom scapegoats. Every time there is trouble, blame lands at their desk. At other times,

Here's an idea for you...

Speak to your child's teacher about giving him a special job that involves responsibility. If the other children see him being a brilliant gerbil monitor or whiteboard wiper, rather than just seeing him as the boy who is sent to the headteacher's office all the time, he is more likely to make friends.

teachers will be aware of the ADHD label but not fully understand what it means, and incorrectly blame poor parenting or interpret impulsivity and inattention as wilful manipulation. One of the best things you can do is teach your child's teacher about ADHD. If his teacher can see he is essentially a good kid with difficulties concentrating and controlling his behaviour, his experiences at school will be much more positive.

STEP 3

Even if your child's teacher is a bigoted, narrow-minded ignoramus, avoid criticising. Your kid is on this teacher's turf for most of the week, and if he knows that you and his teacher don't get on, school life will be much harder. Be tactical. Children with ADHD often do better academically if they are taught in smaller classes. Explain that quiet space to work, both in school and at home, is important; see if it would be possible to include some sessions like this into the timetable. Find out about tutoring options if your child is getting behind with academic work. Many children with ADHD take longer to learn, even though they are bright.

Defining idea...

I had a terrible education. I attended a school for emotionally disturbed teachers.
WOODY ALLEN

STEP 4

Rather than focusing on your child, try to focus on specific target behaviours when talking to the teacher. Talk about possible triggers for these unwanted behaviours and create an action plan to reinforce desired behaviour. Be clear about who will do each task. At the end of the meeting, there should be actions for your child, for you and for the teacher.

Many children with ADHD have additional difficulties. Check out IDEA 30, *Double whammy*, to see if their performance or achievement may be hampered by another condition.

Try another idea…

STEP 5

Set a review date and agree ways you will monitor progress at home and in school. A homework book, school grades and test results are all good ways to track progress. Be prepared to adapt your action plan in light of these review meetings.

STEP 6

You might need to do this through gritted teeth, but do thank teachers for any positive changes they make. Be on the lookout for any times they do things differently and let them know you appreciate it.

Finally, you're unlikely to be the only parent struggling with school challenges, though it can often feel that way. It can be helpful to talk to others in the same position, and there will be someone, somewhere who has been through it too. Ask around – and this is one of the times when a support group can be particularly useful.

If a man does not keep pace with his companions, perhaps it is because he hears a different drummer. Let him step to the music which he hears, however measured or far away.
HENRY DAVID THOREAU

Defining idea…

How did it go?

Q   My daughter is five, has been diagnosed with ADHD and seems bright. She could go to school this year, but would be the youngest in her class. Should she go or are we better off waiting?

A   *Tricky... school might help her develop social skills but if she is already in nursery or preschool, there isn't much to be gained. She might struggle to behave appropriately, given her ADHD and relatively young age for the class. Often a year of extra maturity helps children settle better.*

Q   My child's teacher heard that fluorescent lighting can cause children to be hyperactive and has spoken to me about putting him next to the window and changing to daylight-emulating light bulbs. My specialist says there isn't anything in this. What do you think?

A   *There isn't any evidence that ADHD is related to fluorescent lights, but isn't it fantastic that the teacher's helping? Harness that enthusiasm by offering as much information about ADHD as you can, and by sharing some strategies.*

Q   My eleven-year-old son has just changed schools. He'll have more homework but it's really hard keeping him focused on it now. How can we keep him on task?

A   *I suggest you meet his teacher as soon as you can and explain your son has ADHD and that this affects his attention span, makes him more restless and impulsive. Share some strategies that have worked in the past and see if the teacher has any ideas. Home–school communication is paramount to helping your son do the right sort of planning.*

45

Summing it up

If your child struggles with money or keeping score in games, he or she might have a type of numerical dyslexia.

Struggling with telling the time? Having a torturous time learning times tables? Difficulty with maths often goes hand in glove with ADHD.

Almost all children with ADHD have difficulty with mental arithmetic. Your child may also have difficulty with sizes and proportions. If she has trouble getting the right change in shops or estimating things like distance or temperature, she may have a condition called dyscalculia too.

There's a lot you can do to help. Dyscalculia is a specific learning disability in mathematics. The word dyscalculia comes from Greek and Latin and means 'counting badly' – the word 'dys' comes from Greek and means 'badly', and 'calculia' comes from the Latin 'calculare', which means 'to count'. Dyscalculic children lack an intuitive grasp of numbers and have problems learning number facts and procedures by usual teaching methods.

Here's an idea for you...

You don't need any special equipment to help your child develop mental arithmetic skills. When you're on a car or train journey, practise counting forward beginning with a given number. For example, start with forty-nine and count forward in twos, then in threes and so on. Once you've done this for a few minutes, switch to counting backwards, beginning with a given number – for instance, starting with seventy-three and counting backwards by ones, then twos, then fives and tens, and so on.

Children with dyscalculia find it hard to understand sizes, fractions and recall number order. They also find it hard to interpret mathematical signs and so struggle to add, subtract, multiply and divide. Many children with ADHD have difficulty learning mathematics, but not all have dyscalculia. Whether or not your child does have dyscalculia, most kids with ADHD find it difficult to hold numbers in their head, so mental arithmetic is painful. They are usually able to learn numbers and count on their fingers just as well as other children but when they run out of fingers, or counting bricks are put away, it gets hard. Children with ADHD are typically disorganised and have short-term memory problems anyway, so it doesn't take an algebra whizz to deduce that this doesn't add up to a good foundation for doing sums.

Your child may have dyscalculia if he or she has:
- An inability to tell which of two numbers is larger.
- Frequent difficulties with arithmetic, confusing signs: +,−, x, ÷.
- A reliance on 'counting-on' strategies: using fingers rather than more efficient mental arithmetic strategies.
- Difficulty with times tables.
- Difficulty with mental arithmetic.

- Difficulty mentally estimating the measurement of an object or a distance.
- Difficulty carrying out everyday financial transactions, such as giving change.
- An inability to grasp or remember mathematical concepts, rules, formulae and sequences.

If you suspect your child also has dyscalculia, speak to the teacher and aim to negotiate extra time to complete maths assignments, that your child can use calculators wherever possible and the possibility of working with a classroom partner or teacher aide.

There is some evidence that children can remember numerical things better if they learn them in more than one sense. So instead of just reading times tables, get your son or daughter to read them aloud, while also tracing the numbers in the air with their finger, or better still tracing them in a sandpit or on the beach. They can use this for dates that need to be remembered too. Four repetitions while speaking out loud and tracing seem to work well for many kids. Most classrooms don't have a beach or even sandpit handy, but you can encourage your child to trace numbers with their fingers on a table or desk when they are at school and doing maths. If they have learned tables while tracing the numbers, tracing fingers over a desk can trigger recall during tests in school.

Try another idea...

Children who struggle with maths often have similar struggles with writing. IDEA 9, *The write stuff: improving handwriting*, is a prescription for clarity. Planning time properly may also be a problem, so check out IDEA 27, *Every second counts*, for help.

Defining idea...

Life is too short for long division.
PETER DRUCKER

How did it go?

Q **My son's teacher is not at all clued up about mathematical difficulties. She hadn't heard of dyscalculia and thought my son was just being lazy. What should we expect?**

A *Dyslexia has been much better understood and researched, and many professionals are not yet as aware of dyscalculia as you might expect them to be. Why not see if the school would be open to a talk from a psychologist or special needs teacher with expertise in this field? In the short term, you could show the teacher this. Children with dyscalculia learn best when teachers break down a task into parts and then give step-by-step prompts for each part. Repetition and practice is also much more important for children with dyscalculia.*

Q **My son has ADHD and also struggles with numbers. I am sure he has some sort of numerical disability, but we haven't been able to get this confirmed. I've been wondering if I ought to send him for maths tutoring or to some sort of special lessons. What do you think?**

A *If he is struggling academically, I'd take his teacher's advice on extra tuition. My own view is that it might be better to focus on his strengths and develop his mathematical abilities in other ways. Instead of sending him for extra lessons which could seem like punishment, why not involve him in measuring ingredients needed for cooking, checking the change after buying something or making estimations of distances when you are out walking or cycling?*

46
Speak easy

Many children with ADHD have difficulties with language too. Many don't listen before speaking. Some kids ramble on, others jump between topics before finishing one.

Distractibility means ADHD kids struggle with long instructions and it can be hard for them to shine in class and make good friends. Adults can do lots of helpful things.

Let's tackle some specific areas which are often problematic.

MUDDLED SPEECH

Kids with ADHD are frequently excited about something and want to communicate it in a hurry. The resulting conversation is often a blurted, muddled monologue that leaves listeners baffled and bemused. If this sounds familiar, there are things you can do:

- After your child has told a muddly story, get him to draw what happened on several pieces of paper, and ask him to put them in order.
- Cue him into relating things in a sequence by using steering questions, like these: 'What did you do first at the party?', 'When you got to the theme park,

Here's an idea for you... **Card games are a great way to develop the reciprocity necessary for the art of conversation. Take it in turns to explain the rules and your child will develop listening, attending and turn-taking skills that will eventually help him to speak more fluently and appropriately.**

what was the first ride you went on?', 'Whose idea was it to go on the Zorb roller coaster?', 'What did the firemen say when they cut you out of the crashed roller coaster?', 'What happened next?'.

■ When you are doing a mundane activity with your child, talk about sequence: 'First we'll get the saucepan out, then we'll open a tin of beans, and while I heat the beans, I'll put the bread in the toaster.' It sounds banal but this gives a sense of sequence and structure that your child will pick up on.

LEAPS AND TANGENTS

Impulsivity is a hallmark of ADHD. When kids with ADHD are speaking, impulsivity can show itself in several ways. Some leap from topic to topic, others get interested in something else and are easily sidetracked, many waffle on or focus on unimportant details, alienating their audience. At other times, children with ADHD become impatient, interrupt, talk over others and barge into conversations. If this sounds familiar, here are some suggestions which may help you:

■ Look interested by giving eye contact, nodding and making 'uh-huh' sounds.

■ Encourage eye contact from your child. When he stops looking at you and chatters away, staring into space, ask him gently who he is talking to.

■ Cue your child back on to the topic in hand. 'We were talking about the skate park. Who was skating there today?'

■ If your child butts in, point it out, but try to keep a neutral tone of voice and avoid making a drama out of it.

MISSING THE WOOD FOR THE TREES

Children with ADHD often get caught up on a relatively trivial detail and can miss the main point of something, both in conversation and in school comprehension exercises. Help them develop the attention skills needed to pick up on the appropriate part of a message or story by spending plenty of time discussing what has happened in the stories you've been reading together or in a film you have both watched. Ask older children what they think the main theme was of a book or play.

Reading together is a good way to develop communication skills. Check out IDEA 50, *Reading improves vision*.

Try another idea...

COPING WITH LONG INSTRUCTIONS

Many kids with ADHD struggle to attend to long instructions, and end up missing part of them. At the best of times, kids with ADHD frequently fail to listen before responding and this just gets worse with long questions or complex instructions. Maximise the impact of your message by following a few simple rules.

- When you talk, make sure there are no competing noises like the television going on in the background.
- If you have a small child, get down to eye level and make sure your child is looking back at you.
- Keep your sentence as simple as possible by working out what you are going to say beforehand.
- Smile.
- Check that your child has understood by asking him to repeat the instruction back to you.

I often regret that I have spoken; never that I have been silent.
PUBLILIUS SYRUS

Defining idea...

203

How did it go?

Q   **My ten-year-old son is highly impulsive and often blurts out inappropriate things. He can be so rude, especially when we are out. What can I do?**

A   *Children around that age often use words to get a reaction, whether they have ADHD or not. His impulsivity certainly won't help, but you can modify his rudeness by your response. Be clear with him about what is acceptable and unacceptable, both at home and in public. If he oversteps the mark you should avoid getting riled, but point out it is not acceptable to be rude. Notice when he is polite and does not blurt anything out, and praise him then for being appropriate.*

Q   **My daughter answers lots of questions with 'I don't know'. I suspect that she often does know. Could this be related to her ADHD?**

A   *It may well be. Often children with ADHD have difficulty listening to the whole of a question because their mind is wandering. She might be getting sidetracked, so instead of trying to organise her answer, she bails out and avoids it. I suggest you have a chat to her. Explain that you want to help her structure answers, and that you will try to be more clear in your questions.*

47

What's working?

There are many different tips and techniques. Some are bound to work better than others for your child, so it's important to identify which they are.

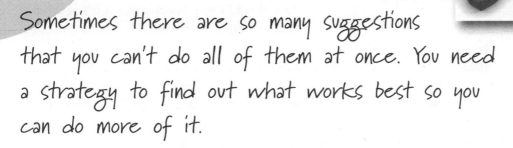

Sometimes there are so many suggestions that you can't do all of them at once. You need a strategy to find out what works best so you can do more of it.

There have been many, many ideas that have helped lots of children with ADHD. But all kids are different, and not all of the suggestions which are out there will work in the same way or to the same extent for everyone. Treatment for ADHD does not just mean tablets but involves a whole range of techniques that you and your child can try at home and in school. With so many different ideas in the mix, it can be helpful to work out whether a particular idea is working and, if so, which aspects of it are working best.

It can all get very confusing, but help is at hand. This is a five-point strategy you can use when you are next presented with a treatment, behavioural intervention or suggestion for your child with ADHD.

Here's an idea for you...

Determine goals in advance and work only on one or two difficulties at a time, such as squirminess, being late for school, and so on. If there is no change in these goals, then the new idea or plan probably hasn't been successful.

GET TO KNOW THE LITTLE DETAILS

Before starting a new treatment or following a suggestion, familiarise yourself with the detail. Ask for a written summary of what is being proposed. If parents or teachers need to do something differently, it's only reasonable that you should know exactly what is being asked, and the rationale for this.

UNDERSTAND WHO THIS TREATMENT OR SUGGESTION IS AIMED AT

Some treatments are just for children with ADHD, others are for children with other problems. It's important to understand which group of children this treatment has been tried on to help you decide if it is right for your child.

KNOW WHAT TO EXPECT

What is the expected effect of the proposed action or intervention? It's entirely reasonable to ask for a list of what is expected to happen as a result of doing something differently.

BEING CERTAIN OF WHAT YOU SEE

It is often difficult to know, impartially, if an idea or treatment has worked. After all, you've probably put in a great deal of effort, so you may not be the most neutral judge of behaviour. In order to find out if you can attribute a change in attention, concentration or impulsivity to a particular intervention, ask someone who sees your child regularly (like a babysitter, perhaps) to observe those three aspects of your child's behaviour before you implement a new treatment or idea, during the time you are using it and a few weeks later. Ideally, the person observing your child shouldn't know when this change in routine is taking place. This can be easily done with some things – for instance, if you are giving medication – but is less easy to do with those like implementing time out strategies or using more praise. Other, more impartial measures of your child's behaviour include school reports and teachers' reports of the effect on target behaviours like sitting still in class, not blurting out answers or interrupting.

ONE AT A TIME

To best determine which ideas are actually working, try only one idea at a time. If you are beginning medication, measure the results of the medication before adding additional suggestions.

Not sure if medication is working for your child? The good thing about stimulant medication is that it works straight away. If you miss a day, you'll soon know if it's having an effect. Find out more about this in IDEA 20, *Drug holidays*.

Try another idea...

Listen to the mustn'ts, child.
Listen to the don'ts.
Listen to the shouldn'ts, the impossibles, the won'ts.
Listen to the never haves, then listen close to me...
Anything can happen, child.
Anything can be.
SHEL SILVERSTEIN, poet and cartoonist

Defining idea...

207

How did it go?

Q **My sister's son has ADHD and she takes him to various practitioners and therapists for all sorts of strange things. She clearly wants the best for him, but it must be so bewildering for both of them. Some treatments are costly and she's not well off. How can she make sure she's getting sound advice and not being ripped off?**

A *You're right to be concerned about your sister and her son. The variety of treatments for ADHD and their changing popularity can be confusing. Unfortunately there are no absolute safeguards. Using the strategies here will help her distinguish between treatments that are scientifically grounded and proven and those that are at best ineffective and at worst potentially harmful. There isn't a magic bullet for ADHD that is the preserve of the rich, so if she's being charged over the odds, she ought to be wary.*

Q **I get confused between all the different terms that get used. What is the difference between a treatment, a therapy, an intervention and a strategy? Is it about the difference between curing ADHD and merely controlling symptoms?**

A *You're not the only one confused about what are at best, merely semantic differences. I use the terms treatment, intervention and idea interchangeably here; they refer to different ways of alleviating ADHD symptoms. Medical professionals distinguish between drug and talking therapies, and would consider both of these approaches to be treatments, or interventions. By strategy, we mean an overall game plan for the battle against ADHD symptoms. There is no cure yet for it, but there are plenty of ways of alleviating the symptoms.*

48

Hearing aids

Listening, comprehension and working memory are impaired in ADHD. This means children with it are more likely to blurt out answers, speak out of turn, interrupt and talk excessively.

Listening practice involves adults giving children positive reinforcement for correctly listening to instructions. It is one of the best ways to help under-tens attend to requests and stop interrupting.

Children with ADHD are easily distracted by noise and movement. Many tend to daydream and seem to be in a world of their own. They may find it hard to focus on one particular activity at a time and also find it hard to follow instructions, which makes learning and socialising difficult. Children with attention difficulties invariably have one of two listening difficulties:

- They cannot screen out what is unimportant so they listen to everything.
- They may not be skilled at controlling attention and so miss large chunks of information.

Spending five minutes each day on listening practice can help. Try to do this at the same time every day. It's a worthwhile investment of time and energy to ensure your words fall on open ears, so follow this:

Here's an idea for you... **Play a family round of Simon Says. This game teaches children to listen carefully for specific instructions and then do the appropriate actions.**

■ Gain your child's attention by saying her name or making eye contact. If getting her attention is a challenge in itself, it often helps to stand or sit directly in front of her, make eye contact, and maintain frequent eye contact during listening practice. Also ask her to stop any other activity she's doing at the time, and to put away any objects so that her hands are empty.

■ Explain that you are going to start listening practice.

■ Maximise the chances of having her undivided attention by switching the television off and doing this at a time when there are likely to be minimal interruptions.

■ Give a number of simple, clear instructions, one at a time.

■ After each instruction, praise her when she listens and does what is asked.

■ Make it encouraging and enjoyable.

Your comments will be something like these:

■ Please put the T-shirt in the laundry basket.

■ Thank you, you're a good listener.

■ Now please sharpen this pencil.

■ What a good listener.

■ Next I'd like you to put the pencil in your pencil case.

■ You're a good listener.

Once she gets good at the clear and simple one-step commands, kick listening practice up a notch by introducing two-step activities like, 'please sharpen your pencil and put it in your pencil case'. Then you can move on to more complicated three-step activities.

Another fun way of improving listening skills is to play sound bingo. Make a bingo card with sounds you would make when preparing an evening meal. These could be things like the tap running, chopping onions, opening a tin or putting something in the oven, for example. Get your child to sit in the kitchen while you cook, but facing away from you. Every time they hear a sound on the card, they cross it off, just like real bingo. It's best if you play with more than one child, as there's nothing like a bit of competition to help them raise their game.

Using a sticker chart in combination with listening practice makes it fun. For more inspiration, check out IDEA 8, *Stars and stickers*. Kids will also be more likely to attend to instructions if they are given in an assertive parenting style, so try IDEA 26, *Assertive parenting*.

Try another idea...

If you have a problem with your child interrupting, introduce a sea shell. At dinner time, or whenever you sit together as a family, when one person is speaking they hold this 'listening shell'. It means that everyone else (including the adults) must listen to what they say.

Another good listening game to play is Champion Distractor, an enjoyable and competitive one. One person has to focus on completing a task, while the person playing the Distractor does everything possible to distract the other person and disrupt the task. In order to win, a person must work hard to be a good Distractor – but also work hard at not being distracted in their turn by other Distractors.

I know that you believe you understand what you think I said, but I'm not sure you realise that what you heard is not what I meant.
ROBERT MCCLOSKEY, American author and illustrator of children's books.

Defining idea...

How did it go?

Q **My son finds it difficult to listen and always blurts things out or interrupts, and I have tried stopping him but without much luck. How can I change this?**

A *It's time to alter your approach. Instead of responding when he blurts out, you need to pause while he speaks, ignore what he says and carry on the conversation you were having before he interrupted. Break the pattern further by looking for opportunities to praise him when he manages not to interrupt and can wait his turn in a conversation.*

Q **My son gets very bored during listening practice. He manages to do the tasks then, but is still interrupting and not listening at other times. Why isn't it working?**

A *It sounds as if it might be that the very clear one-stage commands are too easy. If he can do these, introduce some two- or three-stage commands as well. If his mind seems to be wandering during the five-minute listening practice, have a break halfway through to have a drink or jump on a trampoline and burn off some energy for a minute before returning to the task.*

49

Drawing together

Spending time drawing, painting or sculpting can improve your child's concentration, attention and impulsivity.

Being creative and flexing their artistic muscles can also help children with ADHD express how they feel and deal with emotions.

Drawing can build confidence as it allows children to pursue their own ideas, without any right or wrong answers. It can also serve as a powerful means for developing children's perception and thought. Planning a drawing and developing the skills to complete it helps children with ADHD practise focusing and concentrating. With art as a focal point, children engage in a process that releases creative energy and simultaneously supports emotional expression. Making art relaxes, reduces tension and releases anxiety. Artistic communication is more objective, detached and less threatening than talking about feelings, making it easier to express ideas, thoughts and feelings comfortably. The satisfaction generated from creating art enhances and nurtures self-esteem, too.

Regular drawing develops the following:
- Imagination
- Cognitive skills
- Creative abilities
- Problem solving

Here's an idea for you...

If your child is not confident drawing, why not start with tracing from colouring books? Sit with him for the first one and encourage him at every step. Children with ADHD often tend to be good at starting pictures but are less good at completing them, so encourage him to complete one so that he has a sense of mastery as well as a piece of art.

- Fine motor skills
- Language skills
- Increased levels of concentration
- Social skills
- Focusing
- Listening
- Tolerance

It also enhances a sense of identity and gives a feeling of achievement and pride.

If your child has difficulty holding a pencil or has smudgy handwriting, stick to chunky pencils and crayons. Once he has the hang of these, you can progress to oil pastels and charcoal. Modelling clay is fantastic too. Don't introduce painting until children have mastered pencils or charcoals as brushwork requires remarkable dexterity.

A picture really is worth a thousand words. Specialist art therapists see the benefits of drawing in terms of reduced anxiety and making children feel more comfortable when sharing their thoughts. Drawings have been used by therapists to encourage verbal expression for children with many conditions. For example, a series of drawing instructions has been used to help children with asthma relate their experiences with breathing difficulties and to identify environmental triggers of symptoms. Another drawing protocol using simple body outlines has been used to assess pain severity with children with arthritis. Drawing may help children with ADHD organise their stories and can be a way of finding out what is troubling them.

To encourage your child to pay attention to detail, get him to look in the mirror and draw himself or take him to a museum and get him to draw an exhibit like a dinosaur or insect. Many children with ADHD have topics they are especially interested in, like the ocean or dinosaurs. Structuring a drawing session around a special area can help them focus and stay on task.

Children who lack fine motor skills may find writing difficult too. IDEA 9, *The write stuff: improving handwriting*, has techniques for developing those skills, which can also help with drawing.

Try another idea...

You don't need me to tell you that children with ADHD often have big imaginations. Art can be a safe and playful outlet for their creative ideas and help them practise seeing an idea or impulse through to its natural conclusion. Children with ADHD often struggle in school and life, not for want of ideas, but because they are not able to see them through to completion.

You can develop your child's attention span by getting him to draw a specific object, like an apple. Encourage him to persevere until he is happy with it. You might have to sit through a few dozen circular squiggles until it resembles an apple, but if you both stick with it, he'll have learnt to sit still for longer than usual.

Kids with ADHD like novelty and are more likely to draw spontaneously when there are new materials to explore. You don't need to splash out on an expensive new art set each week, but frequent small treats of pristine sets of new glitter pens or blank sketch pads should get the creative juices flowing.

Art, like morality, consists of drawing the line somewhere.
G. K. CHESTERTON

Defining idea...

How did it go?

Q **I have always enjoyed drawing and painting and looked forward to doing this with my son. Unfortunately he hasn't taken to painting at all and gets frustrated when his efforts are not what he expects. I think some sort of artistic outlet would be good for him, but he is so squirmy and full of energy that he finds it hard to keep still. What might capture his imagination?**

A *Children often like hitting things and some stonemasonry may be just the thing for flexing his creative muscle while burning off some excess energy. Kids who find it hard to sit still to complete artwork may just need another approach. Standing at an easel, lying on the floor or sitting on a cushion at the coffee table have worked well for restless kids I know.*

Q **My son has ADHD and dyspraxia and although he likes painting, he is so messy. He just spreads paint around and smears it into the furniture. I don't think he means to do this, and I'd like to help him be creative, but without all this hassle. Any ideas?**

A *Oh dear, that mess sounds dreadful. I have a few suggestions. In summer, why not get him to paint outside, and wear swimming trunks to avoid staining his clothes? When the weather is cooler, you could switch to crayons or other non-messy art materials. Whatever the weather, please invest in some plastic sheets and mark the paint area with coloured tape, with consequences if he ventures out of it.*

50

Reading improves vision

Some children with ADHD are sold on books while others are daunted by them. Fostering a love of books in your child could be your greatest legacy.

Children who are read to have better concentration, longer attention spans, richer imaginations, increased independence, enhanced communication skills and the greatest range of choices and opportunities...

Nothing rivals reading for its ability to develop your child's imagination and increase his or her vocabulary, the building blocks of thought and communication. Books provide a flavour of other worlds and periods of time, past and future, which are otherwise unavailable. Time spent reading to children every day not only develops their literacy skills, but also strengthens emotional bonds and builds concentration and attention.

Children with ADHD often have difficulties learning to read because they are so easily distracted. One way to understand what this might be like is to imagine you have a tape recorder in your head that periodically skips recording events.

Here's an idea for you...

Some children with ADHD have difficulty getting each eye to focus on the same thing. They may have double vision. If your child says he's seeing double when he's reading or his eyes get tired easily, speak to an ophthalmologist or optician to get a specialist eye assessment.

Over time these skips add up to significant amounts of lost learning time. It is important to try and deal with this and foster a love of books and reading.

One idea is to use public libraries, which are fantastic places. It is quite simple to get a card and, if your child doesn't already have one, I'd strongly encourage you to pay a visit and get signed up. Having a personal card will help your child develop organisational skills – he will need to track his borrowed books and learn to get them back on time – as well as help with his reading.

It makes sense to prioritise library time, so he has time to browse and dip into books, rather than just whisking through. Encourage him to look around and befriend the librarian – and you'll have some free time to look at the books that interest you if the librarian can help your child find suitable books that appeal to him. Many libraries also run author events, puppet shows, craft events, reading circles and holiday book groups, which are all good ways of stimulating and sustaining an interest in reading. Most children find meeting an author thrilling.

At home, get cosy. Children are more likely to sit still and read if there is a comfy corner with good lighting. A beanbag, close to a bookcase and away from the television, is a good starting point.

Don't just think in terms of fiction, either. Give books related to your child's particular interest as gifts. For instance, if he's really into insects and creepy crawlies, a colour reference book of bugs might just pique an interest in words. Regular book buying doesn't have to be costly. Charity shops sell children's books much more cheaply than second-hand book shops. Keep a look out for job lots of books on online auctions. And encourage family and friends to give book tokens as presents instead of money.

Reading doesn't need to be restricted to books and stories. Comics and even magazines can all work their magic. Stick to a principle of reading what children select and you'll find opportunities for reflection and discussion.

Another good thing to do is to take your child to film versions of books he has read. On the way home, chat about how the book and film compare. You can do this the other way around too. If there's a film he really enjoyed, read the book it is based on together and chat about how the film was different. By necessity, film can only contain a fraction of the action or plot in a book and this additional material is a great way of extending the pleasure which often leads on to reading other stories by the same author. Watching *Babe* could prepare your young reader to discover the whole of Dick King Smith's canon.

Try another idea...

Why not incorporate a twenty-minute reading together time before bedtime? If you think you haven't got time, check out **IDEA 27**, *Every second counts*. And too much television hinders development of reading skills. Giving it up could help in many other ways, too. Try **IDEA 52**, *Bin the box*.

Defining idea...

I recommend books with good use of colour. Books with a high picture to text ratio appear less threatening to children. Pictures are useful for building interest and improving comprehension.
SUSIE BABCOCK, nurse and independent educational consultant

How did it go?

Q **My daughter prefers spending hours on the internet to reading. How can I get her to turn real pages instead of surfing online?**

A *Why not spend some time on the internet together, visiting the websites of some children's authors like J. K. Rowling and Jacqueline Wilson? There are lots of interesting activities on these sites – and they are a way of finding out about the books and stimulating her curiosity.*

Q **My son has a limited vocabulary and has been slow to learn to read. He gets frustrated because there are just so many words he doesn't understand and so he gives up. What can I do?**

A *Invest in a good dictionary for children, preferably an illustrated one with great pictures. Every time you come across a new word in your reading together or in everyday conversation, get him to look it up. This is a good way of building his vocabulary. You could also introduce a family word of the week, a game where there is a small prize for the first person to identify and use a new word correctly.*

51

Complimentary therapy

Children with ADHD receive fewer compliments and more criticism than other kids. You don't have to be a specialist to realise that this will leave them feeling bad about themselves.

There are some simple things you can do to redress the balance and lessen the effects of frequent disapproval.

Kids with ADHD often disconnect what is happening now with what happened in the past. For instance, a boy with ADHD may not connect having his leg in plaster for two months last time he jumped off the roof with feeling like playing Spiderman again this evening. Or you might have noticed that your daughter doesn't readily make the connection between sitting down and doing this evening's homework and her end of term school report.

Life has bumps and lumps and ups and downs but, because of this disconnect, children with ADHD tend to see themselves according to the most recent events, rather than building their self-esteem over time. Put simply, if they are in trouble a lot, they will feel bad about themselves a lot. The good news is that the way they feel about themselves can be ramped up and reinforced. Here's how.

Here's an idea for you...

Try to provide as much choice as possible, even if it is whether to eat off a plate or out of a bowl, what colour socks to wear, in which order to watch two rented films.

GIVE COMPLIMENTS

Aim to catch your child getting things right and compliment her, instead of being critical when she messes things up. When you notice her doing something well or simply being good, take a moment to tell her that you appreciate what she is doing.

SAY IT AGAIN

The feedback you give your child can take various forms. Sometimes feedback will be a few words of praise or encouragement. At other times feedback will be a cuddle, an approving look or even just a nod and a smile. Children with ADHD need this type of feedback much more often than other children.

PROVIDE RESPONSIBILITY

Try delegating some simple household chores. Give your child responsibility for certain tasks, like taking the bins out or emptying the dishwasher. Start small with a simple chore like that and create a reward system for completing it. Add responsibility as your child shows increasing ability to complete a basic chore unattended.

BUILD ON STRENGTHS

If your child struggles academically but is good at rowing, for instance, then encourage her to join a rowing team, support her with practice, help her set goals to stretch herself and celebrate her achievements. All children are good at something, so let yours flourish and shine in those areas.

ACCEPT LIMITATIONS

Everyone has limitations so give up expecting your child to be something she's not and instead celebrate her uniqueness and quirks.

SET RULES

Without rules or boundaries, children with ADHD feel out of control. Make sure everyone knows what the rules are – and what the consequences are for breaking them.

Try another idea...

There's little point following all the advice here if it's being undermined by a barrage of critical comments in school. Working in concert with teachers is another good way of bolstering self-esteem. Check out IDEA 44, *School's out*. To make sure the same principles are applied in different locations or with different caregivers, turn to IDEA 12, *Home uniform*.

Defining idea...

ADHD children require these behavioural consequences more frequently than other children. Although responding immediately is important, caregivers of ADHD children must also respond more often in letting ADHD children know how they are doing.
DR RUSSELL A. BARKLEY, international authority on ADHD

CHUNK UP TASKS

You wouldn't expect a child to eat the whole trolley of groceries in one sitting, so chunk up tasks for the week, just as you divide the trolley into regular meals. Chunking up larger tasks into manageable portions will help your child reach a sense of achievement. Let's take an example. Making her own lunch can best be achieved by locating her lunchbox, making a sandwich, selecting a piece of fruit and finding a sweet treat, before making herself a sticky note to put on her bag reminding her that the lunchbox is in the fridge. This sounds basic but is much more achievable than deciding she is old enough to sort her own lunch out and just telling her to 'get some lunch ready for tomorrow', which would probably not work.

Q **I find it really hard to give compliments and feedback. I mean to, then I forget or get distracted myself. And I only notice when something's wrong. How can I break this habit?**

How did it go?

A *Well, one way is to set your mobile phone's alarm to remind you to do so, say every twenty minutes. Keep it on a belt clip and set it to vibrate rather than make a tone as vibration is less obvious to your child. Every time it buzzes, look at and notice what your child is doing and give feedback or praise as appropriate.*

Q **It isn't always practical to give choices – for example, I asked my son where he wanted to play with his ball, and he said 'in the house'. When he makes silly choices like that, I don't feel much like letting him make any others. What do you suggest?**

A *The answer is to set some limits around the choices you present. Try saying something like 'you can play with your ball in the garden or in the park. It's your choice. What would you like to do?' This way he still gets to make a sensible choice, and you have an opportunity to reward his answer with a reinforcing, 'what a great choice'.*

52

Bin the box

Violent television programmes increase the risk of children developing attention problems. For those with ADHD, it might really make sense to bin the box.

Imagine if you could press a button to decrease your child's chances of developing attention problems — the chances are, you'd do it. The good news is you can.

A study published in 2007 by researchers in the University of Washington found attention problems are likely when youngsters watch violent television – the last thing you want with ADHD kids. The Washington study looked at the television-watching habits of over 900 children. They were studied in 1997 and then followed up some years later to see what their behaviour was like. Their parents were quizzed on attention, concentration and restlessness.

The researchers concluded that every hour of violent television that young children watched doubled their risk of later attention problems. Even non-violent programmes like *The Flintstones* carry a risk of attention problems in later life, although the risk is significantly lower than with more violent programmes like *Power Rangers*. These risks only occurred in children under the age of three.

Here's an idea for you...

Turn off the television for a week. Remove the fuse and declare it 'broken' if you're worried about family resistance; if you have televisions in every bedroom and the kitchen you'll have to come up with something more creative. Most families who do this experiment like having their free time back so much that they decide to trash the telly. If you don't want to go it alone, look out for international TV Turn-Off Week, which takes place every April.

One explanation for this is that their brains are at a critical phase of development. Educational programmes like *Sesame Street* were not associated with attention problems in later life.

Over ten years ago, the American Academy of Paediatrics looked at thousands of studies conducted on children and television. They concluded that all of this research has shown primarily negative health effects on violence and aggressive behaviour, sexuality, academic performance, self image, nutrition, dieting and obesity, substance use and abuse patterns.

It's also long been known that watching television is bad for children's physical and mental health. Square-eyed toddler telly addicts learn to speak around a year later than their round-eyed friends. Older kids who watch more than two hours a day have decreased attention spans, poorer memory and recall and are more likely to make mountains out of molehills as they are so used to being drip-fed drama. Lethargy, sluggishness and decreased creativity are hallmarks of children who spend their lives staring at a piece of furniture when they are not in school or sleeping.

In their book *Get a Life!*, produced by the White Dot anti-television campaign, David Burke and Jean Lotus report: 'Most parents say, "sometimes I just need some time to myself and I put the kids in front of the TV for a bit." They think television is helping them deal with the demands of parenting. But just the opposite is true. TV is designed to wind kids up. Frantic cartoons, screaming presenters and loud, multicoloured commercials go streaming into your child's eyes and ears. They come out again with a bang, at mealtime or bedtime. TV spoonfeeds children a steady dose of rapid-fire, happy noises, so they never learn to create their own good times.'

Given the box the boot? And your child is wondering what to do with four extra hours a day? Check out IDEA 50, *Reading improves vision*.

Try another idea...

Many people think television is educational. If this was true, the kids who watched most television would get the highest marks and best school reports, and they don't. Television transmits opinions. Education gives children the skills they need to acquire, make sense of and use information from different sources. Instead of television, try farms, art galleries, museums, zoos, drama workshops and unstructured free time for imaginative play. You may resolve to only watch good educational programmes. But for how long? It won't be long before you and the rest of the household are passively gawping at the rubbish that surrounds the good stuff, and you're back on a diet of junk telly like everyone else. That's not to say that watching everything is bad for you – watching films in the cinema or on DVD has much more in common with reading books, allowing you and your children to consolidate the experience.

It's just hard not to listen to TV: it's spent so much more time raising us than you have.
BART SIMPSON

Defining idea...

How did
it go?

Q   **We're not keen to give up television completely, but we have resolved to stop our son watching violent programmes. But this in itself has caused difficulty. What constitutes a violent show?**

A   *That sounds like a good compromise. The Washington researchers called a show violent if it involved hitting people, fighting, threats or other rough behaviour that was central to the plot or main character. Their list was broad and included* Power Rangers, Scooby Doo *and* The Lion King. *All these shows are very fast moving, and that may also impede children's attention spans.*

Q   **Does this mean that children under three shouldn't watch television but older children can safely do so, ADHD or not?**

A   *I'm afraid not. It's a little more complicated. Although the Washington study indicated the risks of future attention problems were only significant for under-threes, there is also evidence from other studies which needs to be taken into account. The American Association of Paediatrics recommends no television at all for children under two and limited television for older children. My own view is that there are so many good alternatives, there's no reason to press a button that might make behaviour problems worse.*

The end...

Or is it a new beginning?

We hope that these ideas will have shown you that there is plenty you can do to help your child (and yourself) cope with ADHD. We hope you've found some interesting tips and techniques that will make dealing with your child's behavioural problems less exhausting. He or she may still not be able to sit quietly reading for hours on end but you will find your child becoming gradually less disruptive and impulsive.

So why not let us know about it? Tell us how you got on. What did it for you – which ideas really helped to calm your child down? Maybe you've got some tips of your own that you'd like to share. And if you liked this book you may find we have even more brilliant ideas that could help change other areas of your life for the better.

You'll find the Infinite Ideas crew waiting for you online at www.infideas.com.

Or if you prefer to write, then send your letters to:
Calm your hyperactive child
Infinite Ideas Ltd
36 St Giles, Oxford, OX1 3LD, United Kingdom

We want to know what you think, because we're all working on making our lives better too. Give us your feedback and you could win a copy of another **52 Brilliant Ideas** book of your choice. Or maybe get a crack at writing your own.

Good luck. Be brilliant.

Offer one

CASH IN YOUR IDEAS

We hope you enjoy this book. We hope it inspires, amuses, educates and entertains you. But we don't assume that you're a novice, or that this is the first book that you've bought on the subject. You've got ideas of your own. Maybe our author has missed an idea that you use successfully. If so, why not send it to yourauthormissedatrick@infideas.com, and if we like it we'll post it on our bulletin board. Better still, if your idea makes it into print we'll send you four books of your choice or the cash equivalent. You'll be fully credited so that everyone knows you've had another Brilliant Idea.

Offer two

HOW COULD YOU REFUSE?

Amazing discounts on bulk quantities of Infinite Ideas books are available to corporations, professional associations and other organisations.

For details call us on:
+44 (0)1865 514888
Fax: +44 (0)1865 514777
or e-mail: info@infideas.com

Where it's at...